Diary of a BABY BOOMER

MEMOIR AND AUTOBIOGRAPHY

JOHN ALBERT BUCHNESS

ISBN: 979-8-88640-424-1 (sc)
ISBN: 979-8-88640-425-8 (hc)
ISBN: 979-8-88640-426-5 (e)

THE EWINGS
PUBLISHING

One Galleria Blvd., Suite 1900, Metairie, LA 70001
1-888-421-2397

CONTENTS

CANDY

Candy was a white and brown mix of a beagle with something else. She wasn't very tall. Down to the stream and forest we'd go, unless there was snow on the ground. As soon as I got up, or as soon as I got home from St. Matthews school it was down to the stream we'd go- it was 1955. The stream, the field before it Candy and I would cross to reach the trees. We lived on Alameda boulevard in Baltimore with my three siblings. When we left the house for the woods my siblings would be left behind. I don't know what they were doing while I was away with my hands in the stream fetching up polished quartz stones, and being fascinated with the way the stream swirled past. The smell was fresh, and I nearly dared to drink in it, but knew better. This was the city, and who knows how many water wastes were dumped into it from remote sources? At first I went down to the stream and forest without an ax, but my Dad's friend, Jack, decided I needed one, and one evening he came to visit with a brand new hand ax and scabbard just for me! This was the beginning of many peak experiences I was to have cutting trees in the forest, and feeling protected from copperheads that I knew inhabited those grounds. Three, four hours would pass, and Candy would sniff and investigate all the spaces I 'd take her to. There was a pool that collected, and reached maybe four feet deep, that in summer

I 'd wade in and some times jump or dive from the high rock above it. At nine years old I felt like a prince over the lord's lands.

Once when I happened to be with my younger brother Bob above the pool we encountered a teen aged black boy with a pen knife. He approached us wielding the open pen knife in a non-threatening manner, and there ensued some conversation, followed by his direct request for "a piece of ass". Thinking he wanted to carve a piece of our rumps with that knife

I quickly took my seven year old brother away from there *tout de suite*. In our prepubescent minds the prospect of him cutting away at our back sides was horrific, to say the least. When we got back home we wanted to ask our parents why the black boy wanted a "piece" of our asses, but we were too embarrassed to ask and explain what happened to us down at the stream. Of course, as teenagers we were to discover what that meant.

Another day I was above the pool and waterfall when I met a girl a bit younger than I who was terrified and frozen in place by a creature the had landed on her wrist, and just stayed there. It was a harmless dragonfly, and had it not been for a passing adult male smoking his cigarette she might have been imprisoned there. He carefully touched the lighted end of his cigarette to the creature and it took off. I was strikingly impressed with the utility of that smoking burning object. Later in life I would be introduced to the cigarette as a monkey on my back, and wish that its utility extended to dragonfly removal only.

Fast forward to 1957 and I discover like a lot of kids my age the menthol cigarette, in the boys' room, but first in the woods nearby my new home on Staten Island, New York. Dad was a doctor of internal medicine, but he wasn't stationary. He was in the US Public Health Service, and like Army personnel, he was asked to move about every three years. And that brings me to my fourth life crisis, the loss of my best friend, Candy. First I need to tell a few other experiences that didn't include Candy. One day I arrived at school to find a classmate weeping in class. My third grade best buddy, whose name escapes me now, and who sat next to me had lost his policeman Dad the previous night to a gun shot wound from someone who broke into the house. I did not get the whole story, but apparently his Dad surprised the thief, and he shot and killed him. Not long after that I went to a large indoor swimming pool with my school, and a kid drowns in the pool that very day, down the deep end- nobody noticed him. That was shock number two. Still nine years old we're walking close to home on the Alameda boulevard when a kid possibly two years older than I tries to run across the boulevard without looking. He is hit by a car traveling about forty miles per hour, and his cranium is opened up in the road. What a horrible sight. I think I had nightmares for a month after that.

Those were the heavy experiences. I had a girlfriend my age who had some native American blood, Cherokee, I think, and she was interested in me. One of the activities she liked was wrestling out on the field before the stream. That is, with me underneath her. She was strong like a tiger, and when she pulled my hair and pinned me down on the ground I was helpless. I 'm afraid I had second thoughts about her as my girlfriend after that. But I had a boy friend around this time who took me home to his house one day when his mother was out, and he proceeded to take me upstairs and into a walk in closet. Once in the closet he wanted to show me his private parts, and me to do the same. Before he got very far his mother barged in and immediately began attacking me for misleading her son! She ran me out of the house saying never to come here again, and I sat down on the curb and cried, wondering how this whole scene occurred. Needless to say I never set eyes on him again, the little bastard....

Walking home from St Matthews one afternoon with my sister Evie we were stopped by a late model car with Venetian blinds in all the windows. We were asked to get inside and take a ride. A voice inside me said those blinds were not the normal window treatment for a 55 Ford, and we took off as fast as we could in the direction of home. I can still hear baby boomers saying how safe the streets were when we were young!

There was another day when we were visited by a group of kids in various ages who were from the local orphanage. We were down on the field before the stream, and before you knew it these kids were all throwing rocks at us. Some of them were older and could really throw.

One hit me in the chest and it hurt. My group retreated, naturally, and we got away safely. After that we didn't seek out the company of the kids at the local orphanage.

Like I said we left Baltimore for New York in about 1957, and moved into an apartment on the so-called "Quarantine Station" on Bay st. in Staten Island. I'm ten years old, and first saw Elvis on the Ed Sullivan show. I saw him perform "Hound dog" and thought he was the most. Soon I got a 45 RPM of "Don't be cruel", and listened to it non stop. I also listened to the Everly Brothers and tried to sing like them with friends.

Just before our move to the Quarantine Station where my Dad got stationed as a Quarantine Officer, we lived temporarily in a small house out in the country, where we still had Candy. When a couple months later we moved I was told that we would have to say farewell to Candy- she couldn't accompany us to the Quarantine Station. What?! I was told I had to take it like a man, and accept that she'd be put down at the Pound. That she was to be killed so we could move into an apartment that did not allow pets. It was traumatic for me, I did everything with that dog. I think I never forgave my father for that. I felt betrayed.

1946 AND CHICAGO

As I understand it, or was told, I was conceived in New Orleans when my mother was still seventeen years old. New Orleans was my parents' honeymoon, and I was born on November 13, 1946 in Baltimore's Mercy Hospital. My father was still in medical school, having completed college during the accelerated war time program. He was in his residency program when the war ended, and Mom and me were installed in the "Little House", a small unit on my grandfather's property with a wood stove. "Grand doc," as my physician grandfather was called, lived in the "big house" on Newburg Avenue, in Catonsville, Md.. Here we lived for a couple years until my father's training was complete, and he volunteered for the U.S. Public Health Service, which he stayed with for twenty-two years.

Once in the Public Health Service Dad got stationed in Chicago, from where he took an assignment to be ship's doctor aboard a U.S. Coast and Geodetic Survey tour up to Alaska and the Aleutian Islands. After about nine months his tour was up and he returned to Chicago with pneumonia in his lungs. I visited him in the hospital where I was impressed with his deep burgundy bath robe. The artifacts he brought back from the natives were interesting, and I have them to this day, Inuit carved ivory and dolls etc.

My earliest memory comes from this period of my life. When we moved to the hospital station in Chicago off Michigan Drive, we arrived by car from Catonsville. I was pushing two years old and old enough to wear a little boy's white sports coat. I was told that I complained that the trucks passing us "cared me", for scared me. Before my nap I quietly reached for my little sport coat, and flung it out the open window. It must have been summer.

Anyway, I don't think my maneuver was noticed by anyone until it was too late to stop and get it.

I've always been interested in flying things.

One of my fondest and earliest (like I said) memories was napping in my crib in the bedroom of the new house. I remember being fascinated with the light coming through the Venetian blinds, how it reflected warmly on the walls. I remember wondering "what is that?"

I didn't want it to stop.

I started growing along with two new siblings, Evie and Bob, each one year younger than I. And, now at about four years old television had come into its own, with Kookla, Fran and Ollie there to keep us company. Then came Natalie, or Nan as she came to be called, four years my junior. It was about this time that Dad takes off for Alaska leaving Mom alone with four little ones. Here is where I met Jimmy Telfer, my first "best friend." I meet up with him again ten years later, in France in 1960. His Dad was also a doctor on the hospital station. Maybe he was the chief doctor.

School was interesting: on my first day of kindergarten I am on the playground when some older kid (not with our school) proceeds to pummel me with his fists. I think he cut my lip, and off he ran when an adult approached. All I know is that it sure hurt, and I didn't want any further part in school. I think that as a consequence of that beating I have very few memories of my time at Mt. St. Carmel Catholic School. I took a bus, but fought every morning with Mom and the driver, bracing myself in the doorway of the front of the bus to keep from going in.

I learned about the use of force for a second time as they trundled me to the back and inside the bus.

Near the end of the school year I was to attend a play by the older classes, with singing and dancing and a special finale. We, the kindergartners, were set in the front rows.

Near the end of their routine they had one hand behind their backs, and I wouldn't have thought that wax paper could hurt, but when that wax paper ball hit me square in the eye I realized one more time why I didn't want to get on that bus! I think my face swelled up around my eye socket, and all I could think was why the teachers would have arranged an assault on small kids like me, in that barrage of hard paper balls? I remember riding the bus home that day holding onto that paper ball the size of a baseball so I could show Mom what hit me. Of course she didn't think anything about it (?!)

It was about this time that I started to develop the temper that I've had to live with all these years, and be limited by. Dad was home now and out of the hospital, and I guess I was a bit sore about the fact that he left the five of us alone for three seasons, and one night at dinner I refused to eat something-I think it was a hot dog with ketchup, or was it some vegetable like broccoli? (Yuck). Anyway, I got into it with the new "head of the household", who told me I could not leave the table without eating it. So, I told him I would rather leave home than eat that, and he held the door for me as I went out into the snowy evening. At first I made snow angels with my arms and legs, and then tried to sleep in the snow. There was no wind in the windy city that night, so I lay there in relative comfort against the cold. I must have decided after a half hour or an hour that if I stayed out much longer I would freeze to death, so I headed back home in defeat.

Spring gave way to summer and I discovered the Milton Berle show and some cowboy shows like Gene Autrey, Roy Rodgers and Tom Mix on TV. I started to wear cowboy clothes and I got a six gun and holster and hat. I decided one afternoon that it would be a good idea to have Mom's purse with me, along with my holster and gun, and I stole away to go play with the other kids. When I got out there I raided the change purse, taking all the quarters, dimes, nickels and pennies out on the grass. I remember I tried without success to count it up, but at six years old the concept of adding quarters and dimes to the pennies was beyond me. I suppose I shouldn't have considered it so unusual to find Mom out there on the grass with us when her pocket book turned up missing. She insisted on having it back with the change and all, so reluctantly I gave it back to her. After that I felt broke, not an unfamiliar feeling that I'd have frequently in later life.

III

BALTIMORE AGAIN AND PETER PAN

Back to Baltimore and temporary housing in the Little House. I discover with my cousin Steven Jerome that I could fit inside the rabbit hutch, and get stuck there! Nearly. We got out of it, but with a struggle, and the rabbits were cute, and I had always wanted to live like one.

Now there were arrow heads in the earth on my grandfathers property, so we set about to digging a little, but turned up nothing, unlike my father and his brother, David, twenty years earlier, which got them into the local newspaper. Their cache holds about fifty arrow heads and an axe, which I now own under a glass case cleverly put together by my wife, Charlotte, in the past two years.

We soon move into an apartment on North Charles St., owned by a lady named Tarburton who drinks and who reminds me of a witch. Here there is a back garden where my brother Bob and I can play. He is about five at this point, and becomes my companion. One day in this place, where we have a picnic table for a dining room table it's raining, and Mom has found a book about kids and rubber galoshes tramping out in the rain. She read this story to us, an adventure of some kids donning rain hats and coats, and of course their rubber boots, and traveling around town splashing through every puddle. Wow! What an exciting story that I'll never forget. And we did go out in the wet weather with raincoats and boots to get pretty wet, too.

This was the year that the Broadway show, Peter Pan, became a television film starring Mary Martin as Peter, and fantastic it was, with all the props and tricks to make Mary fly through the air. It was Peter Pan for us four kids for months after that. I can still see us looking out the bedroom window at fresh falling snow that glittered like diamonds. With the recent magic of Peter Pan our snowfall became a magical experience that we fell asleep with and dreamed those dreams of childhood only childhood knows.

I got my first bb rifle formed like a pump shotgun, but lacking the interior barrel, so I couldn't get into trouble- it only shot air. This was donated to me by my downstairs neighbor, a former GI about my mother's age, and who had the hots for her. Mom allowed me and Bob(now eight and six) to go to the shooting range with this fellow, John Creasey, who brought his Remington high powered rifle. What a rush to fire that thing! He was a nice guy, and I thought a lot of him after that, even if my Mom was fooling around with him.

Charles St. was the scene of my first temper flare up, and the victim of it was my poor younger brother Bobby. I guess to make the gift of my rifle more equitable Bob received a beautiful jet airliner big enough to hold in two hands. My jealousy was emerald green, and I broke it in half, the beautiful thing. To this day I don't know why I did it, and had powerful guilt from it. Naturally, Bobby was hurt at first, but seem to take it in stride. Anyway, he didn't hold it against me, thank the Lord.

"Some days I'm just tied up in knots" said the subtitle of the cartoon in my father's big book of humorous illustrations. This was one of many books kept in the long bookshelf in the living room. Generally, we were forbidden from these collections, and therefore whenever I could get away with it I'd take several down and search for naked photos or drawings. The "knots" cartoon was about a man literally tied up in slip knots, Picasso style, unable to break free. There were several exciting cartoons with suggestive sketches of women scantily clad and shapely. I would race through this book again and again hoping there was something I had missed. The fuse to my sexuality was lit, and I never got caught. I put the books back neatly when I was finished. There was also a medical book with illustrations of womens' internal anatomy that I found interesting, but it didn't show enough.

Somewhere in the flurry of an abundant home life I completely lost track of school at St. Phillip and James Catholic school. I don't know why, but I have no memory of my second grade whatsoever! No matter, it was time for us to move to the Alameda, and the start of third grade at St. Matthews, away from downtown, and into suburban Baltimore.

It was to this small three bedroom row house we moved and I acquired Candy, my constant companion and my best friend, whom I talked about earlier. Mobility also had arrived in my life with the gift of a bicycle, one almost too big for me. It was time to learn to drive!

Up on the bike and bang down on the pavement immediately were my first attempts, but I soon glimpsed the feel of balance by keeping it going forward, while wiggling the handlebar back and forth. It was unbelievable, the raw power, and unless Candy was with me, I was riding.

I earned a nickel each day that I made my bed, and walked up to the supermarket on Alameda Boulevard for Necco wafers, Tootsie rolls, and my favorite, chocolate covered nougat bars. Not only were my trips after candy bars new but clothes, including gabardine trousers from Robert Hall. My first pair of blue jeans were more important to me than those gabardines for school though, and it was in jeans that I made my very first visit to the dentist. I don't remember the dentist, but I do remember my first experience in the dental chair. I thought investigating inside my mouth was terrific, and as a result I have never feared seeing a dentist since then. It seemed like we spent two Halloweens on the Alameda, and then it was time to move again, this time to New York.

IV

STATEN ISLAND AND THE NARROWS BAY1957

I've already told you about that fiasco of losing Candy, my best friend, in the first chapter. Now we were moving into a three bedroom second floor apartment on the so called Quarantine Station on Bay St., Staten Island. We entered the apartment through the small kitchen, past the dining room, living room, and back to the bedroom I shared with brother Bob. It was a snug arrangement with us boys in the back and the two girls near the front of the apartment, together in their bedroom.

This place was truly amazing. The U.S. Quarantine Station was surrounded by walls and fences on each side of a large rectangle, excepting the front side, waterfront along the New York's Narrows Bay. Looking down from the hill above this little harbor one sees two long docks, one on the right and one on the left. The Public Health tugs come in between the docks and tie up along them. My Dad's job was to get on a tug and go out into New York harbor and board incoming ships, inspecting crew and cargo for transmittable diseases. Their vessels would be quarantined in the event he found disease aboard them. I was not allowed to accompany him, but on shore was a tower with a telescope for identifying the incoming vessels. Up here I was allowed and spent many an afternoon with the watch officer logging in the big boats. After a time I could identify all the Maersk ships as well as the Greek liners that came in.

It was about this time in 57 or 58 that the Andrea Dora sunk off the Atlantic coast waters and had to be hauled back into N.Y. harbor for salvage. What a tragedy for such a modern and beautiful liner to go down. I remember that day on the Atlantic's horizon seeing the tug boats towing her in. This was during the early stages of building the Verazano bridge, which stretched from Staten Island over to the Manhattan peninsula. At this time without obstruction you could see the ending of the Narrows bay as it joined the Atlantic. That was the horizon approximately. We used to hike along the shore line up to the new pilings of the bridge, and watch the great work in progress (as well as play along its pilings). Back on the quarantine station we would sit atop the hill over looking the harbor, and gaze at Brooklyn, its skyline and its buildings. It was directly across the bay from us.

After working up in the watchtower I got invited to come aboard a tug docked in the harbor. It was morning, probably on a Saturday, when I was served the most outlandish breakfast with eggs, stew and beans, and God knows what else. Anyway, I did become very full, and got the impression that sailors had a pretty damn fine life. All of this was going on without the knowledge of my parents. Or, anyone else for that matter. The late fifties were a great time to be kid!

One day a cow washed up in our little harbor, all bloated and scary. How it got there no one knew, but it sure was a monster. Around that same time the Norwegians showed up in their Viking long ship. They were welcomed into our harbor, and all the news people came to report on their transatlantic voyage. These brave young men, who I met and hung out with, were replicating what their forbearers did about a thousand years ago, with the boat constructed according to the Vikings' design. They stayed with us for a couple of nights and were gone.

It was a great experience for an eleven year old.

This was the time that "The Blackboard Jungle" was a popular film, but my schooling was quite a far cry from it. St. Joseph Hill Academy had nuns teaching us, and I and my three siblings all attended this private academy. I say my schooling was unlike "The Blackboard

Jungle" scenario, but aspects of the social life surrounding it were familiar. Part of the walk home, after descending the public bus was fraught with highway men! I guess we stood out with our white shirt and tie, and neatly pleated navy slacks, so we had to run a gauntlet to get home some afternoons. One neighborhood had this nasty kid who enjoyed first taunting me, then beating on me. I was not able to defend myself against this brigand, and had to jerk myself free then run, which I managed to do without being beaten bloody. It was pretty constant for a time, then he left the scene, and I made it home without interference from then on.

Back then it was fairly common for kids as young as seven or eight to ride the public conveyances alone, and I at ten was no exception. Another thing that was common was for us very early to buy cigarettes and experiment with them. Nobody knew if you weren't buying them for your mother, and nobody asked. I remember buying Salems(yea, menthols, cool) to try after climbing over the station's fence to reach a little wooded area nearby. I guess I bought them at Sam Beulah's store on Bay St. The experience was fairly disgusting I recall, and I didn't feel all that well for some time afterward, but that didn't prevent me from experimenting further. That's where it began, and so many miserable years of that monkey on my back followed. I finally kicked the habit when I was about forty five years old. There were many periods of abstinence, sometimes for years, but I kept coming back to it.

"Splish Splash, I was takin a bath" sang this guy, Bobby Darin, and what a powerful impact that bath had on me. I went to bed with that song in my head, and until the "Purple People Eater" came along a little while later, it was Bobby Darin I wanted to get to know. Now here was a rival to Elvis. And, little did I know it then, he was to have an even greater impact on me about two years later.

"Bucky Fucky Beaver," brother Bob answered when Mom was putting him to bed. What?! I only know that I sang that around Bobby earlier that day, referring to the Ipana toothpaste commercial featuring Bucky,Bucky Beaver. Mom was not happy, and Bob took the weight for it. At eight he learned there were words you just didn't say, and "Fuck" was one of them. Life went on, but somehow our bedtime kisses just didn't seem the same after that.

Right outside the Quarantine station one day I got knocked out by a kid I hardly knew who sucker punched me for no real reason, perhaps an exchange of words about nothing, I don't remember. I was down on the ground, but got right up with an awful pain in the jaw.

I was momentarily unconscious, the kid took off, and I don't think I ever saw him again.

Another time I was visited by two school mates, David Neville and Austin (his last name escapes me). Around the side of my apartment building we moved when David pushes me on the ground and Austin proceeds to kick me in the torso. They beat on me a while and then left saying something like I hope I learned my lesson, or words to that effect. Nothing was said about it back in school, and oddly enough David Neville later became one of my best friends at St. Joseph Hill.

I was at this time waiting only for my eleventh birthday to arrive, so I could matriculate into the Boy Scouts. As I requested repeatedly my Mom bought me the Scout Handbook, and I devoured it cover to cover, as they say. Soon I'd be walking down Bay St. to the American Legion Hall on Monday nights for my scout meeting: Troop 181, NYC, with Mr. Palermo our Scout Master, and Kenny Wagner my Patrol Leader.

When I wasn't singing Everly brother songs with my friends in the church yard next door to the station I was dreaming about Boy Scout life, working on merit badges, and going on marches and camping outings. I remember that first twenty mile hike, how exhausting it was, but how great an experience! Joe Palermo was a world war II veteran, and a widower, who lost his wife in a car accident. Consequently he was automobile phobic; he refused to travel in a car, so when went out of the city on camping trips we rode the bus to the ferry, and on to our charter bus.

On Friday nights in the summer all the kids of the Quarantine station were together playing a hide and seek game called "Olly Olly in free" in which we hid among the buildings like the monkey house. Yes, monkeys were kept for apparent experiments in a laboratory building, off limits to us of course, but useful for hiding behind. During the endless summer days I enjoyed lying and staring up at the blue sky, for what seemed like hours. We had a serious swing set and practiced jumping high from them. In more secret hours I'd get under the bushes with as friend and experiment with wanking, to use the British expression for masterbating.

The hours were long in the summer, as they actually were all year round, and I got my first job up at the Army base, Fort Wadsworth, and the end of Bay St. I set pins on weekends in the bowling alley for ten cents per hour and a coke at the end of the night. This was a time before automated alleys, and I would often sweat back there in the heat. There was no air conditioning, only fans, and it did get hot at the end of the lane. You had to gather up the fallen pins and put them in the rack to set them down on the surface, but in a hurry, there wasn't time for breaks. It was constant labor for about three hours. I got good and tired.

When winter came it was time to go down to the pond and ice skate and play ice hockey. I got my first pair of hockey skates, they were brown and black, and made me feel like I could go 60 mph. At first it was hard developing the ankle muscles to hold the feet upright, but it didn't take long. Soon I could manage a stick and shoot the puck where I wanted it to go. It was two seasons I recall we were skating, and except for being chased by the notorious Walkewitz twins, whose territory we had to cross through to and from the pond, we had some of the best times of our lives.

When summer came around again the family packed up the '55 Dodge station wagon for Vermont, to Lake Spotford, near the New Hampshire-Vermont border. It was there we had our large aluminum row boat, from which we fished and water skied. I was able to use another wooden row boat for rowing, which I did with obsessive regularity. I do believe I developed great forearms and pectoralis majors from it. After several weeks we were back at home, and the long hot summer dragged on in the city, with visits to Sam Beulah's store, and to all our friends in apartments on the station. Down to the docks I took my rod and reel and cast for hours, sometimes catching a striped bass when they were running in the bay.

Back at the Scout troop my Dad was installed as troop doctor from the very beginning of my membership, and I was very proud. He didn't do much diagnosing at our meetings, but attended whenever he could. The time had come for us to move, as usual Dad was taking on a new position, this time at the Public Health hospital in Stapleton, a couple miles north on Bay St. We moved to a huge house on the stations grounds in late '58. At least it seemed huge compared to the apartments we were used to. I could still walk to my scout meetings from there, but it was time to break with old friends and start again with new.

THE HOSPITAL, STICKBALL AND BOBBY DARIN

Brother Bob and I got the third floor bedrooms with a window overlooking Bay St. After this move I rated a radio, so I soon was able to listen to the Allen Freed radio programs, with all the rock n roll I could want. My best friend at school was a diminutive youth named John O'Shea, and with him I learned all about the NYC bus system, and rode the bus to and from school, and then over to John's house, where he lived with his two sisters and his father. His mother had died some years earlier, and his older sister had pretty much assumed the mother role, she being several years older. John and I would ride the bus from school on Friday afternoons to the ferry terminal where we'd buy a fresh baked loaf of Italian bread and eat it til we were stuffed. We hung out at the ferry terminal and some times used the recording booths to try and sing some rock hit, for me preferably the Everly Brothers' songs. It cost about fifty cents, and would let you record about three minutes. Naturally, the audio quality was severely limited, and our brief encounter with recording sounded kind of funky. But it printed us a 45 rpm disc to take with us. I wonder today how many of those we made, and what became of them? It was truly magical, state of the art, and I was blown away by it.

On the hospital station I became friendly with the Chaplin, a Catholic priest, and agreed to serve mass with him in the early mornings. So, I got up about five AM and several mornings a week went to the chapel, wearing a white robe of some kind, to be a proper altar boy.

It was very solemn, and I enjoyed it for the most part. I didn't like the father's body odor, though. He smelled moldy, like he had only one pair of slacks, which he wore without ever washing them.

My Dad was treating patients now at the hospital, while we played stickball in among the buildings and lots of the hospital's grounds. I loved stickball and could play it for hours on end. All that you needed was a wooden rod and a small rubber ball a bit smaller than a tennis ball, and someone to pitch it to you, with or without bases, it was a minimalist game. The hospital was surrounded by grassy lawns including a baseball field, so we also played baseball, mainly on Saturdays, when we had all afternoon.

Dad wanted me to have an entrepeneurial side, so he carpentered me a nifty snowball cart to wheel down to Bay St. on warm days, with an assortment of syrups to go in the shaved ice cups. The ice shaver was the most interesting part of it all. The shaver was a razor blade positioned like a carpenter's planer, and it filled up in the back of its small box, enough for a good sized snowball. I took my ice down to the bus stop on Bay St. and sold my snowballs for fifteen cents each. One day I earned seventy-five cents, or five of them sold.

I made friends with the son of the hospital chief, Bobby Bowden, neighbor in the next house across a lane. He was the same age as I and he introduced me in a big way to Mad magazine, and we would spend hours reading back issues and current issues, laughing at every nuance. His interest in rock n roll was not like mine, but he always made me feel at home when I was with him in his house.

In the summer after my seventh grade I went to Boy Scout camp in upstate New York for two weeks. I had inherited a valveless bugle, and had "Taps" and "Reveille" down, with some part of "Volare". When I got to camp I heard the designated camp bugler morning and night, and in between playing Volare for real. He sounded like Vivaldi with his phrasings; I decided to put away the bugle, at the camp at least. The days were occupied with latrine duty, which consisted of sweeping out the crap with a net, dumping the proceeds to a hole in the earth, not an amusing task We got a lot of swimming and some skinny dipping in for good measure. I was working on my carving merit badge when I sliced my thumb big time, but it didn't require stitches, and sure was an inconvenience. One night after dinner we had an initiation ceremony that went like this: we stood before a group of leaders who asked us to repeat the following Indian chant: "HoWa ta Nass Ah Yam" We chanted for what seemed like an hour until we were pretty tired of it. When the meaning of this "Indian" chant was revealed I felt pretty stupid indeed. In English it read "Oh what an ass I am". So much for initiations, I thought.

Almost every day I wrote via post card to my Mom, and I am sure she appreciated that. I never mentioned the initiation.

Between the time that I was eleven and thirteen I suffered a phobia of death. Going to sleep at night I was afraid it would be my last, perhaps influenced by the Christian prayer "Now I lay me down to sleep....I pray the Lord my soul to take" et cetera. I've always wondered if such a depressing thought shouldn't be the last of a child's nighttime routine. One morning I was abruptly wakened by a head first fall from a very tall building (maybe the Empire State that I visited). In any case, it was the closest I had come to dying in my young life, and wow, I was shaken for a couple of days after that dream/nightmare!

I was starting eighth grade and by that point I was the single remaining boy in the school choir. I was the only bass, and still interested in the choir. I was also quite interested in girls, so I was content to have them all to myself! It was about this time that the school started having sock hops outside when the weather was warm. A DJ ran the records and we danced, something I found I had a real talent for. So I danced with the girls, and found one very special girl, Pat Larson to be my special girlfriend. She was blonde, of Scandinavian descent. We had a relationship since seventh grade, and I would bus out to her place with John O'Shea, but we never got to make out, either from her fears or from mine. The other problem was that we were always with someone, either her girlfriend or my friend Johnny. I guess it would have to be enough that I had the prettiest girl in my class.

About this time Bobby Darin re-entered my life with his hit sensation "Beyond the Sea". I bought the 45 rpm record and nearly wore it out, dancing a routine in front of the mirror, and attempting to sing along with it. It was a very sensuous experience, and it made me wonder what it would be like if *I* were really performing the song!

On December 14, 1959 my twin brothers, Alec and Neil, were born in the hospital where we lived. I don't think Mom knew she had twins until the birthing moment, and they were identical, and premature, so had to be incubated for a time. We were soon walking them and playing with them. This time Mom had a lot of help, with the four of us around to care for them too.

It was also during this period that I was first confronted with a real horror. It was '59 I believe when the Nimer couple were murdered in their house, allegedly by their eldest son.

He is supposed to have stabbed them to death with a hunting knife while they slept in their bed. Their other two children did not witness this, being asleep, and the house was locked from the inside, making it difficult for detectives to assume an outsider. The reason this nationally broadcast event came so close to home was that our next door neighbor, Dr.Mack Smith, took the young boy into his home immediately afterwards. He was only eleven years old,. Dr. Smith was a Mormon, and felt obligated to take him in. I am not sure if the Nimers were Mormons or not.

He was kept under close supervision, but I felt afraid with the proximity of it. We were all encouraged to pray for the boy, but I had trouble getting to sleep for a good while. I understand that the Nimer boy, who is now in his sixties, denies the crime to this day, and no other suspects have ever been found. The Nimer family lived about a mile away. The case is unsolved.

On Sundays our family all attended Mass together at the local church, "Our Lady of the Sea"on Bay St.. After Mass my Dad had the tradition of dining out, and sometimes that meant traversing the bay on the ferry for Manhattan, and Chinatown, for a big meal. We each ordered and shared the entrees all together. It was enough food for a platoon of soldiers. Fortunately, dining was cheap in those days, so with six kids in tow, we all ate until we were bursting. I am afraid I got kind of chubby from it, too.

Now Elvis, Paul Anka, Frankie Avalon and Fabian all had pompadours, so starting with seventh grade I discovered Brylcream, after some time with butch wax and crew cuts. Hair spray became a favorite borrowed item from the girls and Mom. By eighth grade I had trained my hair into a proper two inch high pompadour. Mine was more like Paul Anka's. Elvis's was hard to emulate, but his was the "toughest." It certainly attracted the girls, and like I said, I had the cutest girl in the eighth grade, Patricia Larson.

In June of 1960 I graduated from eighth grade with a lot of pomp and circumstance. The year before I was confirmed, and took Michael for my confirmation name, after St. Michael the archangel. I didn't know that I was practicing a form of spirit worship, and I guess until I was about thirty five I must have believed in angels and their providence over us human beings. What a fantasy world Catholics inhabit!

VI

MAISON LAFFITTE 1960 L'ERMITAGE 12

Well, it had been three years, and it was time to pull up stakes and head to a new world, this time to Paris, France. Dad got the position of Quarantine Liaison for Western Europe with an office in Paris. So, before June had expired we were aboard the SS United States, of the Cunard line, a brand new ship. We were booked first class, and the accommodations were dazzling, with matinee movies in the morning and baked Alaska in the evenings. We had a swimming pool, and we frequently dined with the ship's captain. Swimming was very important to me, having attained my swimming merit badge last year and having achieved the status of Star Scout. I really thought I was to become an Eagle scout, but like with my dog Candy, I had to leave a lot behind me, as we moved into our house in Maison Laffitte, seventeen kilometers southwest of Paris. However, while Dad was looking for that place we stayed with the family of Jimmy Telfer in their "Chateau du Sable" or castle of sand. Remember Jimmy Telfer from when I was five on the hospital station in Chicago? Yes, he was now taller than I and well versed in French. He took me on the train into Paris where we visited the stamp market and the Left Bank, and dined at nice restaurants, where I first had wine and steak au piovre. It was life at the top, for sure. Girls were the only thing lacking, but soon Jimmy came to the rescue with his two teen aged sisters, who were particularly attractive, especially completely naked. He had devised a way to watch them showering through a hole in the wall in his bedroom. It was very exciting, especially knowing that they *didn't* know!

My Dad took over the job Dr. Telfer vacated, Quarantine liaison et cetera, and the Telfers were on their way back to the States. We moved into a house in France's big horse racing town, Maison Laffitte, at 10 Avenue Voltaire. Dad bought a new beige Peugeot station wagon, which I thought was great. Our new home had a front and back garden, and four bedrooms on three floors. It was deluxe, and heated by a coal fired furnace in the basement, which I, now thirteen, was appointed the caretaker of. That meant that in winter I got up before anyone else, went down to the cellar, and shoveled the coal into the furnace. It was hard to get up early, and the coal and shovel were heavy, but a part of me said I had a good job, so I did the best I could. Next door to us to the left was a house with stables full of horses, and consequently the smell of horse manure. But it was exciting, and despite the language barrier we had tea with our new neighbors, at around four in the afternoon. Their house was neat, what I saw of it, being only in the kitchen and a small room, and these people raised and trained race horses!

In the fall of that summer 1960 started a new school year in a private school called "L'Ermitage", about a fifteen minute walk from home. In my case, though not at first, I rode my Raleigh racing bike, received a couple of Christmasses ago on Staten Island. I remember taking this bike from the hospital station miles away, out to the highways and forested areas on the Island. It felt like real freedom to a twelve year old. I was glad I got to bring it with me to France, but I found out that kids my age had motorbikes, which brings me to my first unsuccesful business venture.

Between my sister Evie and me we had a 45 rpm collection of about fifteen records, the latest hits from American rock n roll, most purchased from a record store on the north side of the Island, not too far from Tompkins public swimming pool. There I spent many a summer day diving off the high dives, which were really high, about twenty feet, I think.

But, back to France, and I was introduced to a French girl, a friend of the Behrends twins, Eric and Christine, who had a delapidated older version of a Mobylette to sell me in a trade for our rock n roll records. I thought that was greatest deal in the world, and took home the motorbike my father forbade me having: "motorbikes are dangerous," he said. I did get it running one time, but soon gave up. Boy, was Evie pissed, and I thought about getting the records back, but no dice. The deal was permanent, I had a lemon on my hands and the ire of my father and my sister.

Thank God for the Americans, Eric and Christine Behrends, who attended L'Ermitage with us, and who taught me most of the French I learned. It was very convenient too that the twins were both in my class, roughly the equivalent of ninth grade, so I had ready interpreters when I needed one. They had been living in France for a few years, so spoke fluent French. With them helping me I became conversational with French in about six months.

At age fourteen languages came easily to me. Not so with my core subjects. My pursuits were countered by another American, who unfortunately shared the desk next to mine, and enjoyed wiping his boogers on me. He was a tall Jewish kid from California named Dick Sears.

He was essentially a bully, and my ninth year in school soon turned into a nightmare.

Dick was left in this boarding school by his parents, ostensibly to learn French language and culture, while they remained in California. Because of his size he intimidated me, while acting as though we were best friends. Frequently he pinched, punched and twisted my arm for attention. His sinus was always running, and the outgo from it was truly disgusting and constant.

He seemed to carry a cold all the time.

My grades were failing, all of them, and by the end of the year I was declared a total failure in my academic pursuits. I could never manage algebra and geometry in French, and soon gave up. Well, Dick was the American bully, and there was also a French bully named

Bonnuit. He must have weighed two hundred some pounds, was tall, and picked on my brother, Bob. I, being a bit larger now, was not intimidated by him, and in fact had an altercation or two with him to get him to leave Bob alone. Alas, he kept it up the entire school year. Evelyn and Natalie did pretty well, and didn't have bully issues to deal with. The twins, now a year old were cared for by Mom and her live-in maid, Aletheia, from Spain. There was a serious language barrier, in that Aletheia spoke neither English nor French, so most communication was improvised, and a Spanish dictionary was necessary to poor Mom.

One night I got up to go pee, I think, in a sleepy state I returned to my bedroom, or what I thought was my bedroom, and turned right into Aletheias room. I got into bed with her, half asleep, and then maybe fell back to sleep. My father must have been awakened, and came in to hustle me out of there. I don't think it even awoke Aletheia, but it was made very clear to me that I was doing wrong trying to make love to Aletheia in the middle of the night. Boy, was I embarrassed, and tried to defend myself, but my Dad wouldn't buy it. To him I was *guilty* as charged. For me it was traumatic; I had simply made a wrong turn, and ended up in the bedroom next to mine and Bob's. It was so bad I believed that I had unconsciously crept into her room for lewd purposes, although now I realize I hadn't any such intentions. I took clothesline and tied my ankle to the poster of my bed for the next few nights. Everybody knew of my *faut pas*, how

I was trying to fuck big fat ugly Aletheia. Even my brother and sisters were informed! And it was one of those cases where your father thought that was what you were doing, and so you believed you must have been at that, too. Months later I stopped believing it, though, and came to realize it was just my father's Victorian mind set that made him accuse me. However, I think that to his dying day he maintained that accusation was accurate, or justified. In any case, the incident caused a deep rift in my relationship with him. That same disturbed relationship carried well over into my manhood.

Thinking back to the first days of French school I, or maybe I should say we, got a shock when we were required to participate in physical education: On a cool morning in October we were asked to run about three miles. Yep, without stopping-impossible! I detoured into the woods until they came around for the second time when I caught up with the class. They had us dress in shorts in that cool weather! Yes, the hardy French. Good thing I hadn't started smoking for real by then. I had had eight years of no exercise to speak of, and then track and field big time! My poor lungs just caved in.

On Sundays we four went to the movies, or to the "cinema" as it was called here.

It became our habit to go into town to the matinee that started about two o'clock. So, first to Mass at St. Nicholas, then a meal, and then off to the cinema, to see "Spartacus", and some of the nouvelle vague (new wave) French films.

After school we would sometimes go into the town of Maison Laffitte to stop at the bakery for French bread "baguettes" and dark chocolate, also sold in the shop. We made a sandwich of the bread and chocolate and then we were in heaven all the way home. What a wonderful experience that was. It was on our way home one afternoon that we first met "Malabar" our Algerian friend, who approached us on his racing bike. He was friendly and shy, very curious about Americans, and especially my sisters, Evie and Nan. His dark face and black curly hair identified him as one of France's minority, the Algerians. Using our fledgeling French we became fast friends with Malabar, and we would hang with him often when were in town.

Our two years in France was neatly divided up between the 1960-61 school year and the 1961-62 school year. We transferred in our second year to the US Army run school at Garches, France. They came and got us in a big orange school bus. It was then I first met Phil

Dandino, who would introduce me to my soon to be best friend, Jean Louis Stringer, a French boy of Maison Laffitte town center, and son of a Gendarme. Philippe, Jean Louis and I were all the same age, about fourteen, though I attended the American high school with Dandino, while Jean Louis of course went to the local "lycee," or French high school. Phil was blonde and a very popular kid among the Americans and the French community of kids. He played the guitar, and rather well, actually. He brought it on the bus to school, and then I received my first guitar lessons. He taught me "The Wanderer" by Dion de Mucci, and possibly a Roy Orbison tune. Phil's father was a

U.S. Army Sargent married to a French woman, and therefore Phil was bilingual.

We had been over to England in the Spring of '61, London and Stratford en Avon, visiting the Shakespearean sights and Hyde Park.. On our way back home we bought a guitar for Mom in Holland, with steel strings that stood a quarter of an inch off the neck, and was impossible to play, though I tried, and figured out a couple of things when I wasn't picking up Phil's guitar (which was nice). Dad got us a German radio and we could tune into Radio Luxembourg, but sometimes broken up. We got Chuck Berry, Jerry Lee Lewis and many of the black groups that were popular Stateside, and of course the Everly Brothers and Elvis, who was now living in Europe on his Army tour of duty.

The summer between the school years we traveled by car through Germany and Spain, and then on short air flight to the island of Mallorca for a two week vacation. In Barcelona my Dad bought me a hand made Spanish classical guitar, which is now in possession of my oldest son, Danny. The Barcelona we visited was that of General Franco, Spain's dictator and president. There was much evidence of a military leadership, with marching soldiers and checkpoints. In Mallorca it was quite different and the Mediteranean Sea was warm and welcoming. At night, at dinner we were entertained by a guitar duo who knocked me out. I don't remember what they played, but all of it was great, and after listening to the Kingston Trio record given me by Dr. Mack Smith the year before I was fascinated by the beauty of a small group. I think they played "Sleepwalk" by Santo and Johnny, and I later learned that one on the guitar. One night while we slept Gypsies took down every piece of clothing from our clothesline, including our bathing trunks and suits, so we had to go out a buy new ones. I remember traveling on the bus into town, and the passengers apparently did not use deodorant. The whole bus smelled of body odor! It was hot there, but it was a dry heat, and it didn't aggravate you.

It was with some sadness that we left that paradise.

I don't know if it was my haircut or what, but back at the new American high school tenth grade held the usual for me: new kid at school, and you guessed it, bullies, again. My first days in tenth grade were plagued by this very Aryan looking senior who was tall and well built, and who took it upon himself to police new kids, I guess. My first encounter was at an assembly where I stayed well to the back of the auditorium, but he came back there to find me and manhandle me. He meant to scare me, and certainly succeeded in that. I steered clear of him after that, and he ignored me, thank the Lord.

I struck up a wonderful friendship with Jean Louis Stringer, pronounced "strand-jherre". I met his Mom and Dad, where the three of them lived in a small apartment, his bedroom decorated with record cover photos of Elvis. Jean Louis had a new blue Mobylette with a seat long enough for two, so when I was with him I didn't have to pedal. I would buy him light blue wrangler jeans at the PX, and he'd look cool and American, and was very grateful for them. He paid for them, of course. One day we hitch hiked up to Camp des Loges, the Army installation where the Post Exchange, or PX was. It was about ten kilometers or more away from Maison Laffitte, near a place called St. Germain de Pres.

On the way home we had some trouble catching a ride, and we had walked a good distance. I don't know what got in to him, but Jean Louis decided to hock a lugee on the next windshield coming past. They (two guys about thirty-five years old) decided they didn't like that, and stopped and came back to where Jean Louis just entered the forest and could not be found. I, on the other hand, was a little slow to realize what just happened, but I took off for the forest too, as they began to exit their vehicle. They ran after me and caught up to me. One of them picks up a log and starts hitting me in the face and head with it. It was painful, and they kept up their beating me until I reached a state of semi consciousness. They dragged me into their car, and that last thing I remembered was coming to on a sidewalk on the outskirts of Maison Laffitte. I don't remember being dumped out of the car.

I walked down to Jean Louis' house, and bruised and bleeding explained to him and his mother what had happened to me. We had tea and I got cleaned up, and then went home.

Once I got home I started planning my revenge on the two. I built a pair of brass knuckles out of old piece of metal I found in the basement, very carefully shaping it to fit my hand. I have never felt such severe compulsion to hurt someone. The next week I went out to the place where they dropped me, and started searching the environs for their car. I found it! It was outside an apartment building, and it was early evening. The reality hit me that I was where I was, and it was possible to commit murder here! I changed my mind, I mean I suddenly came to my senses, and decided my plan to kill these guys was stupid, and that there was a chance I could get hurt.

I left in a feeling of defeat, but also of relief. I made the right decision, but Jean Louis let me down. He let me down because he left me with them, and didn't stand and fight. But, what could he have done? They were twice our age and no doubt twice as strong... they would have hurt us both. But, why did he have to spit on their car? Did he ever say he was sorry to me?

I don't know, but I realized that even a cop's son could do the wrong things.

Our life riding the bus every day was where we discussed our lives, and made our plans. It was about an hour ride, and there were girls that kept it interesting. There was a little making out, but it was kept to a minimum. Phil had Deanna, and everybody knew they were

steadies. There was a brunette on the bus I wanted to get close to, and I think we made out once, but it never developed. One afternoon on the way home Phil invited me over to his house, and we joined up with Jean Louis, where we made french fries and café au lait. It was great, and Phil had gotten a new record called "Please, please me" by an English group whose name I didn't catch. Much later I remembered that day that I heard the mysteriously beautiful song, and thought to myself, "that was the Beatles!"

In the house next door to us lived a pair world war II widows, but I didn't know that until after Jean Louis got me into my next batch of trouble. We decided we needed to get into bomb making. We bought fertilizer, and Jean Louis told me that if we joined sugar with it and ignited it we would have nifty explosive. So one morning we put it in a lead pipe with a sugar fuse, set it up in the back garden, lit it and got out of the way. Boom! It blew a hole in the ground where we laid it, about half a foot deep, and the pipe was shredded all around.

Right afterwards we heard some women screaming next door. Now this was not long after the Algerian crisis in which the Algerian military threatened an air assault on Paris. A gendarme soon showed up at the house asking what we did, and he recognized Jean Louis as the son of his co worker. That much was fortunate, so we didn't end up in a lock up. He warned us not to do that again, and told us what a fright we had caused the old ladies next door. Phew, close call!

On another day Jean Louis and I took a girl he knew on the back of the motorbike, and me on my bike, out to the forest with a liter of beer. Well, when we got into the woods, and had a few sips, and offered her a few sips, we soon drained the bottle. I felt too inhibited to do anything with this attractive young woman, and I guess Jean Louis picked up on the vibe too, so we just visited there in the woods, and had a good time talking, and we soon came back to town.

That was the end of that adventure.

In the Spring of 1962 there was a party announced at my school, where we would stay overnight. I went to the shop where I knew I could buy some cooking brandy, and so got a bottle of that and hitched my way to the girls house. Some of the sophomore class was in attendance outside in the forest near the girl's house. It got dark and we lit small fires, sat and drank. I drank my whole bottle of cooking brandy, and soon felt sick to my stomach. But I was OK to sit for a while kissing the girl who invited me. It was not long before I was crashed in her lap, and I only remember waking up at dawn on the cold ground all alone with a new sensation, a hangover. I hadn't drunk brandy before, especially not cooking brandy. I found out it was not for drinking, the hard way.

At school someone had told me there was a stolen Vespa scooter left somewhere in the woods nearby where the party was, so on my way home I made a search for it. Sure enough, and not far from the road, was the scooter on its side, but undamaged. I lifted it aright, checked for gas in the tank, and started it up, and I was on my way home with my own transportation. I stowed it in the woods by our house, hiding it quite well. It was behind the German bunker left over from the war. Little did I realize just how illegal my act actually was.

Soon I was, however, to fall into bad company.

There was a boy on my bus and in my grade who used to talk about leaving windows unlocked at school so he could come back at night to break and enter. One day he approached me with a plan to steal another motorbike. I had told him how I found my stolen goods. He wanted me to meet him about two AM one morning, and to carry him to the place where he would swipe a motorbike. Not thinking is a facet of going on fifteen, and I agreed to the crazy scheme. I climbed down from the second floor window of my bedroom in the hotel we were now living in, since we were about to board ship and return to the States later that month. In order to pack up our belongings we moved out of the house and into the hotel nearly across the road. Anyway, David, I will call him, and I, snuck away from the hotel area, mounted the Vespa, and took off that warm night to an apartment building near Garches. I parked and David went into the basement with his tools to remove the hinges from the storage bin where this brand new Mobylette was kept. How David knew it was there I had no idea.

A short while later he came out pushing the bike silently toward the roadway, and we were off undetected within seconds, back to Maison Laffitte, and back to bed. Dad was doing his career ladder thing, and we were to board the S.S. Independence in June of 1962. I got wise and dumped the Vespa far from home, and although we rode the bus still I never found out if David's was a perfect crime or not, since we left France at the end of the school year. I suspect he was found out, and always felt guilty about my part in the heist. As usual, however, we were packing and moving along, this time to Washington, D.C.

VII

NAPLES, ITALY THE SS INDEPENDENCE AND HOME

With the station wagon loaded with a travel rack on top for luggage we said goodbye to our friends and neighbors, traveled South, staying in hostels, and traversing a lot of beautiful countryside. We made our way through Switzerland and into Italy.

We passed through Milan and made it to Florence, where our true vacation began. Many times I had visited the Louvre in Paris, but now the squares in Florence were like outdoor museums, not to mention the many museums of art works. I recall seeing a Michaelangelo statue of David outside, but I was later informed that was a reproduction, and that the real statue was somewhere inside a building. It was spectacular, nonetheless.

We stopped for a day or two in Venice, and I loved St. Marks Cathedral and square, and the glass blowing pieces I saw in the shops. The gondola ride was also a treat.   We moved on to Rome and saw all the sights like the Coliseum, and neighboring

Pompei, with its ancient pornography which impressed me no end. All those erect penises in pictures and in sculpting were amazing! The restaurants were fantastic, all that pasta and tomato went down wonderfully, and always different from dish to dish. I really liked the road they call the Appian Way. I gazed out the car window constantly at all the fields and trees as they passed.

Finally, we were in Naples, Italy's home for poverty, and the southern Italian seaport of the Mediterraneum. There were sailors walking everywhere, and I visited a department store with Mom. Walking between the apartment buildings I was impressed with the sheets and laundry hanging on lines from one side to the other. With the sea breezes blowing I was surprised the things didn't blow off from the lines, but I guess Napolese women know just how to attach them securely.

We boarded the SS Independence in Naples, and were off across the Meditarraneum to the Atlantic for four days of pleasure. Bob and I met two brothers roughly our ages, who turned me on to Turkish cigarettes, called Sobranis. Their tobacco tasted so pure, compared to French cigarettes. We hung out with the two brothers at the swimming pool, and now I was pushing sixteen years old, I was old enough to visit the lounge and see the live entertainment. It was all well and good, but I couldn't help but feel I had left behind a lot of friends and beloved places. Another thing, there were no girls my age on the ship. Quel domage!

I recall coming into New York Harbor, seeing it in the early morning hours, and thinking about the first passengers of the first ships to arrive here. It was a fascinating thought, how it must have felt to be a teenager arriving in the new world. three hundred years ago.

"Catch a falling star and put it in your pocket, never let it fade away" was the sound of New York when we left in 1960. Perry Como was certainly popular still at that time.

Arriving there in 1962 was a different world altogether. Elvis had come back from Germany, and was fast putting out a new sound with "His latest flame" and "Little sister". Soon the Beatles would return from Hamburg, and the Shadows were playing guitar instrumentals that thrilled the London and European publics. John F. Kennedy held his "Camelot" court with first lady, Jackie.

A youthful spirit dominated the United States, and the space age and space race had begun in earnest.

We brought back the Peugeot 503 with us, and I am not sure if we ate dinner at the Horn and Hardart family restaurant, before driving on to Baltimore to be with Grand Doc.(John Adam Buchness,MD) We might well have, for it was my parental grandmother's family business. Catherine Horn Buchness died while bearing my youngest uncle, Michael, when my father was just sixteen, and left him a small fortune she inherited from the Horn family. His new mother became an African American maid named Grace, who substituted as a grandmother to me, and to my siblings and Buchness cousins. Grand Doc never remarried.

It was summer in Catonsville, and the evenings were spent watching theater presented for television on black and white TV. The Twilight Zone was still going strong, as well. We had sleep overs from the Phipps family, my cousin Ruthie, in particular, snuck into my bedroom and we became kissing cousins in between drags from the few Sobrani cigarettes I had left. The Phipps were my aunt Charlotte's family, my Mom's sister, three years older than she. Her second eldest daughter, Ruth, and I were closer than cousins should be, and I learned the pleasures of French kissing with her.

"The hair's gotta go" was the message I kept getting from the adults around me.

My double pompadour, I was told, made me a "juvenile delinquent", whatever that was. It was "double" because at the time I had it going back on the right and the left. Brylcream was my secret weapon. Aunt Joan Buchness said I wasn't welcome round her place unless I got a haircut, and my Uncle Howard Phipps chased after me one night at a party with a pair of scizzors! He never caught me, hah!

VIII

BETHESDA 1962-1964

Dad had been promoted to an administrative position in the National Institutes of Health, NIH, in Bethesda, Maryland, and he and Mom were busy finding us a new home there. A three bedroom house on Battery La., in what was a nice community called Battery Park, became our new home. It had a rec room in the basement, and a comfortable living room, with an outdoor porch attached. It was all brick, a handsome Georgian style home. This time he purchased the property, which had a back garden, that bordered on the community center's grounds, with a clubhouse. Hey, does that mean we break the three year residence rule? Nope, by summer 1965 we'd be moving to San Francisco, California. More on that later.

In the Fall of 1962 my sister Evie and I entered Bethesda Chevy-Chase High School, while Bob went to Leland Junior High School with sister Natalie, AKA Nannny.

My early memories are of the wide American streets, which seemed enormous. My first day as a junior in high school was thoroughly alienating, the crowds, the size of the buildings were intimidating. There must have been thousands of kids in this new school! I became very small, indeed, and frightened. We'd walk the approximate mile to BCC, past the Hot Shoppes, where students with cars cruised around the drive in with intercoms to order a coke, or milkshake, and maybe a hamburger. Compared to Maisons Laffitte it was all *too* big!

I threw myself, along with brother Bob, into decorating our new bedroom in a two tone beige and brown paint, brown on the base, beige above. We were determined to paint it all

very precisely, with the window sills and trim in brown. It was all very beautiful when we finished. We were very proud.

I was still fifteen starting the junior year, and this was the age I got my first real job. Auburn Esso was a Standard Oil line pump station where my Dad bought his gas, and got to know the proprietors, Sam and Maurice Gendleman. He must have approached them about me, because my Dad told me to go there, a job was waiting for me. And, sure enough I went there and a job was there for me, pumping gas and washing windshields for 1dollar an hour. Now, this was a "Service station" where we all had to know about cars. There was a full time mechanic, Lefty, who could educate us, if we asked him to. I learned a lot about engines and car problems in a short while. I also became "tire man" for part of the twelve hour shifts I'd work on Saturdays and Sundays. That was the beginning of my lumbar back disorder, I think. Hefting those heavy tires on and off the cars was too much for the fifteen year old growing spine.

In November of that year I turned sixteen, and I wanted a Winchester .22 caliber

lever action rifle. I felt old enough, and I guess my father agreed with me, so I went up to Western Auto on Wisconsin Ave., and brought home my prize. It wasn't long after that my Dad

also bought me a 16 gage J.C. Higgins shot gun from Montgomery Wards.

I worked through that summer seven days a week until school started, then went part time on weekends.. It was hot hard work, with changing and fixing tires, and other small tasks assigned by Lefty, out thirty-eight year old hero. It wasn't long before I came under the influence of more bad company. I met Jeff"Peewee" Noah, and then another kid whose name I forgot, because frankly I wanted to forget him. He worked with me on the weekends, went to Bladensburg High School I believe, and he played the electric guitar, apparently for some time.

Peewee went to BCC with me in my grade, but regardless of his small stature, was a natural leader, who was a member of the "Saints", a much coveted club(/gang). They were all popular athletes, with their club logo on their letter jackets. They were also arrogant snobs, but Peewee was all right, and he seemed to get along well with everybody. It wasn't too long before I entered Peewee's inner circle, and was made aware of how to take home some extra money by slipping a buck in my pocket from one dollar gas purchases. It was easy, and everybody did it, including my friend the guitar player. He told me I could buy a Fender guitar and amp from a man he knew who sold them "wholesale", and he encouraged me to save up my illegal earnings for one. At first it was hard for a Catholic school boy to participate, but it got easier, and it wasn't long before with my regular wages I had enough to buy a Fender Jaguar electric guitar and a Princeton amp. I went to his friend's apartment in the neighborhood, and found a brand new Fender rig waiting for me. I paid him my savings and took the goods home with me. I'll never know for certain, but even then had the inuitive sense, based on the price I paid, that these goods were not really from a legitimate dealer.

I was soon ready to rock and roll, and my brother Bob had two brother friends who wanted to form a band, Eddy and Bill Roche. So with Bobby singing the lead, Eddy on guitar with me, and Bill on drums we had a garage band out back. I learned "Wipeout" and "Pipeline" and then some James Brown songs that Bob wanted to sing. It was slow starting, but we soon had a repertoire, and the "Profiles" were born. We practiced after school until we were called for dinner.

At this time Bob and I used to stay up until eleven to watch the "Steve Allen Show". He was the world's funniest man, we thought, and once he had Elvis on the show.

When school started we had to get to bed earlier, and that was all for Mr. Allen.

At school I had an English teacher named Mr. Nathan, and he had our attention by giving us stories and work that was meaningful. He turned us on to an autumn story by William Saroyin about a boy and his shotgun, and his coming home with a bird to eat. I don't remember much more about, but it took place around Thanksgiving, the season we were in while we were reading it. "Our Town" by Thornton Wilder was another one I loved. Eleventh grade English was fun. Not so for Algebra, and I could not keep up at all with the class. The teacher cared little if we paid attention or not, and kept it powerfully boring. Come summer I had to go to summer school to take Algebra over, and had a fascinating young teacher, who explained it as a language, and made it fun. I ended with an appreciation for Algebra, and got a B. I actually looked forward to going home and doing the homework! It all depends on the teacher.

I met my best friend about this time, after Thanksgiving. Brian Norcross became a dear friend, who was already driving at sixteen. He had a younger brother, Chip, and younger sister. They were nice. Brian was a member of something called the "Isaac Walton League", which meant he was a serious fisherman, and he took me fishing whenever we could. We used to go down to the Potomac River, and out to a place called the Isaac Walton Club, where there was a small lake. He had his own car, a '56 Chevy, so getting around was no problem. One time we bussed downtown Washington, DC with a few dollars to shop clothes in some special shops he knew about. We visited the burlesque theater while we were down there. I came home with a nice sweater. It was deep green. Brian confided that day that he had been abused by an adult when he was a bit younger. I'd never known anyone who that happened to.

A little later this year my sister Evelyn and I attended a speed reading course, by the Evelyn Wood institution. We walked to a place on Wisconsin Ave in Bethesda, and there we were introduced to some primitive hypnotism techniques to help us with the act of speed reading. While in the nearly hypnotic state we "scanned" the page rather than read it. I am not sure the course made me read any faster, but the technique of scanning the page for the overall meaning was helpful.

Intramural wrestling was my next big thing, and I found a great joy in after school sessions of rough and tumble. Not actually on the

Wrestling team, it was the next best thing, and I learned the holds and how to compete. Along with my new found interest in wrestling I rather enjoyed a late afternoon class called Music Appreciation, where we listened to the great symphonies and had some discussions, but mainly we listened, with many falling asleep, to the chagrin of our aging teacher. She was a sweet old lady who tolerated a lot from us.

I'm not sure if it was the spring of 1963 that I first heard the Beatles on the radio, with "She loves you", which became a number one hit. Some of my peers considered the new band a bunch of "fairies", but my first impression was nothing other than other worldly. I had never heard anything like their music, and I eventually loved it. Our little combo, the Profiles, later learned "All my Loving" when it came out. Like the Beatles we loved the Isley Brothers' "Twist and Shout", and like them we learned to play it, along with "Surfin USA", by the Beach Boys.

I think Charlotte Daniels entered my life about this time. This folksinger, who with her lead guitarist, Pat Webb, were popular in downtown DC, but somehow came to be friends of my parents. They were in their thirties like my parents, and were frequent visitors to our home. Charlotte sang and played the guitar, and I remember her performing "In the Pines"and "Nobody's business" in our living room with Pat, the boss guitarist whose mastery of the blues made their LP very special, indeed. I still have that record, and still listen to it. The Kingston Trio and Mitch Miller singers were my first couple albums, prior to my discovery of the instrumental group the Ventures, whose hit "Walk don't run" was a smash hit. Their LP of the same name was on the record player nonstop. I loved the Ventures, and we did their big numbers like "No trespassing,"to the best of our ability. The Battery Park community clubhouse was our very first venue, and we had a great time playing the dozen or so tunes we knew for dancing teens and adults.

One day on my walk home I chanced to see a black 1949 Ford Coupe convertible at a service station along Wisconsin Avenue. I inquired about it, found out it did not run, needed a lot of things, including a carburetor, and maybe a clutch. They wanted forty dollars for her, so I came back with the cash, and somehow got it home either by tow truck, or by improvising the engine parts, to get it to move. I don't think I checked with my father before I brought it home, but I guess he thought it was a good deal. At least he didn't tell me to take it back. I got busy working on the convertible, first fixing the ignition switch which was defective, then took off the carburetor and proceeded to rebuild it, following the instructions that came with the rebuild kit.

Now this was a flat head V8, and was fairly straightforward to understand. It needed plugs and new points, which I installed, but I had trouble setting the points right, and the carburetor rebuild didn't take the first time round, either. I despaired at first,but then starting asking the right questions, got her running. The Ford occupied the forward portion of the drive way just before the garage, and my father's other car occupied the middle part of the driveway.

He had bought a late model Mercury with push button automatic transmission. This was before I had a learner's permit or anything, and one night when he and Mom were out I decided to take the keys and try to take it for a spin. I started it up, put it in reverse, and before I knew it was nearly airborne into the railing of our basement stairwell. What power that big V8 had!

God, was I scared! I drove it back forward into its space, got out and started thinking about my next move. I had none. All I knew was that I had dislodged the railing from its concrete base, and was in world of trouble. Well, he wasn't happy, and I was punished by delaying my driving permit for about a year, or until I turned seventeen. When everybody who was anybody was already driving it was the worst punishment I could have gotten. From there I relied on Brian

Norcross, and my new neighborhood friend and classmate, Tommy Haywood, for rides. It wasn't so bad, I had a lot to occupy me with my part time job at the station, fixing the Coupe, and playing in the band. Anyway, I still snuck the '49 Ford out and drove it without a license, or tags or anything, just to feel the road under me. One evening after I was out with it Mom and Dad came home about the time I was returning, and caught me red handed. After that I didn't take it out anymore, but was content to work on it in hopes of the day when I could get it legally registered and all.

My dear mother had paid for guitar lessons for me at a music store up in Bethesda, from a guitarist who he said had studied with guitar great Charlie Byrd. He started me on ukulele books learning the chords to standards like "Dozy Doats and Mairzy doats", "Try a little tenderness", and others. It was boring for the most part, and I quit before long. I wanted to play rock n roll, but at this time had heard a little classical guitar by Andre Segovia too.

Chuck Berry was big, and nobody could play like him, not even the Beatles or the Shadows.

As the junior year came to a close in June '63 I was firmly established at the gas station part time until summer, when I could work full time. I met a new boy at the station, who drove a 1953 Plymouth, and whose name escapes me, but he was a good buddy, and he took me out to Dickinson Quarry for swimming and diving. It was to the west out past Rockville, and was once a working stone quarry. It was a beautiful place, and I loved diving from the cliffs. Yeah, the quarry was a real turn on, and I only wish I had kept up my friendship with that mystery coworker who gave me such a gift.

My Mom used to pack my lunch up until my senior year, when I used cash to pay for lunch. There was a lunch room affectionately called the Alibi on Wisconsin Ave near the movie theater. They served burgers and fries topped with gravy, and it was *the* place to go among the cool guys of the school. The Saints and other club guys all congregated in the Alibi. It was just a matter of getting back to classes within the half hour break we had for lunch, which was frequently quite a rush. I can remember eating while running back to school, but the food was good, greasy spoon style.

IX

SWAN ST., THE PROFILES STAN AND ANNE 1963

Summer '63 had arrived, and it was time for the Profiles to get busy practising for teen centers and parties. A country boy from rural Pennsylvania came into mine and my brother's life at the end of the school year, Stan Zyvith, a tall blonde Pollack. He was in Evie's class, and he lived not too far from us. He had the use of his father's Pontiac, a really fast car.

I wish I could say he was a good influence on us, but alas, he was the son of an alcoholic he loved dearly, and who let Stan go his own way, bad or good. Funny enough though, it was that we were all students of Sunday school Catholic Christian doctrine, at Our Lady of Lourdes Catholic church on East West Highway in Bethesda, learning about Paul and the road to Damascus. This was something Dad wanted us all to attend, and though I resented it, and was bored by it, I didn't violate house rules, and every Sunday after Mass I was in the class room. I don't remember a thing about it, but Stan was a sometimes attendee. Stan was an avid fisherman and hunter, and we would travel down to "Cabin John" along the Potomac River, about twenty minutes from Bethesda. Bob and I had our own rods and reels from our earlier life in New York, so we were set. One Friday, a weekend that I didn't work, we somehow got permission from our parents to camp out down on the Potomac, and got into Stan's vehicle, and found a small beach along the river.

This trip was one of many we were to take fishing with Stan, and the banks of the Potomac became our second home. We set up a comfortable camp, and before long it was dark, and we sat by the fire watching the stars and the water, with our lines in the water passively waiting for a bite. It must have been about eight thirty when we heard the shots ring out, and felt the projectiles flying through the trees just above us. Stan doused the fire, and instructed us to lie down near the tree line and be quiet. Adrenaline was pumping full in us when we slowly hear the thrashing of leaves, and the approach of a yelling young man coming down to our camp site. Stan confronted him on his arrival, and told him to take it easy with the 410 shotgun. He was obviously a drunk eighteen year old red neck from Cabin John, or thereabouts. He gave us his name, but it's been long forgotten, and we invited him to sit with us before a fire. He insisted on shooting his rifle into the water, making a lot of noise. He told us we all had better behave like he wanted, or there'd be trouble. He had a box of 410 shotgun shells sitting by his side, and he sat on a log just outside our circle in a way that he could control us with his weapon.

Well, our visitor remained rather incoherent, and it got late, and I wanted to go to sleep. So, I did, or so I tried to do. He made it difficult, with a variety of threats against us.

Around two AM he fell into a drunken slumber holding his gun in his lap. First Stan and I and Bob discussed what we were going to do, then decided to sleep. We awoke with the first rays of dawn across the river. He got up too, but it appeared with a hangover. We brought in a fish or two and fried them up, offering our guest some. After that I went down to the river bank to wash up. I bent over to splash my face when, pow, I felt a hornet sting below my calf. I saw the water splash up near me too, and realized I'd been shot! Apparently the buckshot went through the water before it penetrated my leg, so the wound was superficial. He stopped shooting when I complained I'd been shot. I cleaned the wound, and the pellets did not penetrate my leg. He was pretty badly hung over, so Stan and I knew he'd soon doze off again, so we might rush him and take the rifle and ammunition. It took about an hour but sure enough he fell back to sleep, and Stan managed to steal the box of shells from him. When he came to, he was aware of the missing box and threatened to shoot us if we didn't give it back. He had one shell chambered in the rifle, and he pointed it at Stan. Stan talked him down and negociated an exchange. He told him he would return the box of shells if he unloaded the shotgun, which he agreed to do. When he unloaded the gun Stan pretended to give back the shells then rushed him, stripping him of the rifle and overpowering him. The three of us surrounded him, and he, in his hung over state submitted. We took the single shotgun shell from him, and proceeded to pack up our gear.

When we were sure he was without ammunition we returned to him his rifle and took home the shells with us, and didn't look back. It was a rough night, and I didn't get much real sleep, so I was glad to get back home and to bed for a nap.

One Saturday evening as I was about to work out with the Profiles my father offers me a can of beer, so I thanked him and drank it, which made me feel quite high. I played my guitar like never before. I had no idea what this beer would cause me in the next year. That night I had no desire for more, but in the succeeding weeks and months drinking beer became a focus of my life, and the weekends became a nonstop search for an adult buyer for the me and the boys I was with. Now the drinking age in Washington, DC was eighteen, and it was only twelve minutes across to the DC line, so it was easy to find someone eighteen years of age or more, or some one with a fake ID. Drinking beer was cool!

It was another Saturday night and I was out with Stan Zyvith, and of course we had some beer, and Stan's father's car. It was time to cruise the streets of Washington. Now I still had a lot to learn about my buddy Stan, and we were pretty inebriated by about eleven.

We were out of cash, and we wanted more beer, so while we are driving close to a curb Stan asks me from the driver's seat to open the glove box. Out of it he produces a pistol, and he points it at the guy about to enter the crosswalk. He tells this gay man about forty years old to hand over his money. This very effeminate guy takes his last three dollars out of his wallet, and hands it to Stan, who then speeds off. Stunned, I asked Stan why he did that?! He simply said "because we needed the money." I asked him if he always kept a handgun in the glove box. He responded simply that "it comes in handy, doesn't it?" We bought more beer, went back to Bethesda, and then home. What a night!

The law and we were destined to get together, and yet another Saturday night found us very drunk out toward Rockville and a residential area. For some reason we got on one another's nerves, and we stopped the car, got out on a front lawn, and started to duke it out.

The police were called by the home owners to get us removed from their front lawn. We were taken to the lock up in Bethesda, and because we were minors no charges were made, and our parents were called, but not before we were cooled down by the cell for about an hour or more.

I suppose I was grounded for a while, and told not to be drinking. Another close call!

Losing my virginity was a full two years away the night the Lefty took us all downtown in his Lincoln Continental, me, Peewee and somebody else, to a Swan St. location, to be graced by the black whorehouse he knew. It was a warm August Saturday night, and we'd all just completed a twelve hour shift at the station. Lefty had bought a case of beer, and we helped ourselves to it, at the station, and then in the car on the way downtown. He announced we were all to get laid, and we took off. I was very excited and when we arrived on Swan St. there was a pimp outside the house, and Lefty approached him with a tip, and he led us all inside,

There were men and women walking about the house, laughing and drinking. We were offered a shot of whiskey each, to gird up our nerve, I guess. I remember it was harsh, and burned my belly when it went down. My seventeenth birthday was two and a half months away, and I was the youngest of our crew, and I definitely felt junior, with handsome Lefty in the lead. He went into the back bedrooms first, and I waited, now intensely anxious, wondering if I could really go through with this. I looked around at some of the ladies, and became even more tense. I saw the men exiting the back rooms with talcum powder on their hands, from where they'd been washed up by their lady. That clinched it for me- I wasn't going in, and just politely refused. Peewee looked funny at me and asked "what's wrong?" I said "no, nothing's wrong I just don't feel like it." He knew I got cold feet, but didn't say anything. We all left together, and drove back to Bethesda.. It was funny, but back at the station following that night nobody ragged on me about it. I'm sure because of my age I was spared any ridicule. If Mom only knew I was out with her gas station boyfriend that night. It was obvious she was attracted to him from conversations she had with him when she got gas, but whether it went any further I'll never know. I wonder what she'd have thought about the lessons Lefty was teaching me other than car repairs! ***

I met Anne Dorris when sister Evelyn had brought her over to our house one afternoon, and the two of them were hanging out in the living room. I met her, and then went my way. I wasn't much impressed with this brunette, who could pose for vogue magazine with her natural beauty. Nobody then could have told me that she would be my wife for sixteen years and mother to two of my children!

THE DEATH OF
KENNEDY, DATING

I was entering my senior year of high school in September of '63, and school just didn't hold much interest for me anymore. I spent time with Brian Norcross, fishing and going to movies and the like. I remember one afternoon with my Fender Jaguar and amp we worked out a version of Ricky Nelson's "Travelin' Man," with Brain singing. He did it well. Brian was a frail sort, or so it seemed, before that day after school when the big fight was announced between Brian and another kid at school, who challenged him. It drew a large crowd, and Brian stepped right up to the presumably superior opponent and with one punch knocked him out, or at least down to the ground, and that was the end of it. He was declared total winner, having bloodied the other's nose, and apparently broken it. Anyway, Brian was served a reprimand from the school authorities, and threatening notices from the other boy's parents to involve the police.

From then on Brian was no longer frail, he was a hero!

I was in woodshop class when it was announced over the school intercom that President Kennedy had been shot that day in late November. That was a real shock to me, as Kennedy was dear to me, the young President with such positive energy. He represented youth and the future to most of us young people. It was a great loss.

I had finally gotten my driver's license as promised after my seventeenth birthday, and so got my '49 Ford Black with white top convertible tagged and legal. I started driving to school-what power I felt! It was shortly after that I started traveling down to the Picolo Tavern on lunch breaks with members of the Saints. A couple of draft beers and a hamburger, then rush back to school for gym class, half drunk, but happy, with a sense of belonging. Nobody ever asked for ID to see if I was really eighteen.

I don't remember exactly when was the first day I "hooked" from school, but during my senior year I had about twenty-five days of absences that were not excused. I don't know how I graduated, and my grades were in the D range, for everything except French. I never studied for French since I spoke it fluently. I found a partner to hook school with in Bobby Humpreys, who hated school like I did, and we spent the mornings and afternoons together, doing who knows what? Most of our school day was spent walking from place to place aimlessly.

My weekends were spent drinking at the Picolo, getting really drunk. One night my father intercepted me coming home to the house, and threw me in the cold shower with all my clothes on! I think that was the time he realized something wasn't right with me, and he started me going to Bethesda Naval hospital to see a psychiatrist. The doctor said I was depressed with anxiety, and gave me Librium. I liked the effect of the Librium, and it did seem to help. I never drank when I took the Librium, but I continued to drink, which was the cause of my problem.

One night we bought a case of beer and headed out in my convertible towards downtown. I let one of the boys drive my car, Dick McAllister, and that turned out to be a big mistake. He stripped the transmission of its cluster gear, blew first and reverse. We were all drunk and didn't care, however, and rode around until late. The next day when I was sober again Dick offered me twenty-five bucks for the car which was useless to me, and I took it like a fool.

He probably got it running again and made it a fine set of wheels once more. Anyway, I didn't see him anymore after that. My drinking had reached a point where I didn't care much about anything. The quick sale of my car proved that.

Fortunately I started seeing Anne on dates which began with us going out to see Alfred Hitchcock's "Psycho" at the local movie theater. I remember it scared us, but we got over it shortly. Nowadays young people see that movie and think nothing of it. At the time, 1964, there were not many film experiences that were so shocking. I started spending my Saturday nights with Anne, and one time we got a six-pack of beer out of a car near where we were parking, outside an apartment building, so we moved to another dark and secluded location, and drank the six-pack and made out. It was the first time a girl touched my member and brought me to an orgasm. Anne was the horniest girl I ever met, but we kept our sexual experiences to petting and kissing. Sexual intercourse was out of the question, being too risky for pregnancy.

Anne was a junior and a year younger than I, but she was already driving by age sixteen, and often had the use of her father's Chrysler Imperial, which was in a class by itself.

The thing had power steering, which was way different from our Peugeot station wagon, which I painfully took my driving/parking test in. The 1963 Imperial was spacious, and you could stretch out and lie down in the back seat. What a luxury vehicle! Her Dad was also a doctor, and a General in the US Air Force. Need I say he was intimidating?

Anne and I started to meet more often, and we played tennis together at the community center courts, next to our property. Coming back in from tennis we went up to my bedroom while both parents were out, and lay in bed cuddling. One afternoon she climbed on top of me and humped me with our crotches tightly held together. I think I came in my pants that day.

My senior year carried on, and I stopped skipping classes so much when I was with Anne. My twelve grade English class was full of hooligans, club guys and worse, who would make fun of Mrs Marquez for some reason. I never understood how they could humiliate her the way they did, and I learned nothing from that class, it was so disrupted. Poor Mrs. Marquez would be crying by the end of class some days. While I rarely saw Anne at school, the influence she had on me was good, and the frequency of our after school meetings increased.

.I had stolen my sister's best friend from her, but little did I know that just four years later we'd be married in a wedding that was not approved by her parents. She was model beautiful with full breasts at sixteen years old, she was everything a guy could want!

Still, there was another girl I was chasing, Carol Howard, a steady to one of the Saints, Chad Allen, I think it was. She lived over in Chevy Chase. She had auburn hair and a perfect figure like Anne, and I think I was after her for her body, and the fact that she was a club girl. And, she looked like Brigitte Bardot. I still went down to the Picolo with Mark Mc Intyre and other Saints on lunch hour, coming back late for gym class, but it was great to get a couple of beers with my new found friends. I was never invited into the Saints because one of their requirements was that you lettered in some sport, which I did not. Clearly, the best athletes at our school were members of the Saints, with few exceptions. Jim Street was one: a star football player, he was not in the Saints, but hung closely with them. I knew him from my junior English class, and became friend to him. He was tall and robust, and he played End on our football team.

LOUIE, LOUIE, 1964 COLLEGE

The Profiles kept at it, and by '64 we had played teen centers and dances. "Louie Louie" by the Kingsman was one of our favorite songs then, but we sensed the coming changes with school ending for two of us, Bill and me. It meant the Army helicopter corps for Bill and college for me, though I wasn't interested in college. I was more used to drinking beer by this time, and didn't get drunk all the time, but still spent Friday afternoons down at the Picolo.

My Dad kept me seeing the psychiatrist at intervals, and I think it helped me. I saw no game plan for myself, and wasn't sure what I was going to do after high school. There wasn't anything I wanted, except possibly to be with Anne. My father was the wiser, and he arranged for me to be admitted on probation to his alma mater, Loyola College, in Baltimore. I don't know how he got me into the all male college, but it was (forgive the pun) just what the doctor ordered.

My high school graduation was like everything else about high school, a going through the motions, and I think I must have worn shorts and a tee shirt to it. I walked down the aisle and got my diploma, not knowing how I had achieved that. All in all, it was a great load off my chest, and now I was free to quit the service station, and take a full time job at the Glen Echo Amusement Park down by the Potomac, off

River road. I was made hip to this, naturally, by somebody in the Saints. I got hired to manage the Skee Ball, a dime for three balls. I took with me a Webster's dictionary, and some paper back novel about a depressed n'er do well, who is possessed by thoughts of suicide and drinking. I vowed I would read the whole dictionary over my summer in down time (plenty of that), and I think I must have worked twelve hours a day; I couldn't remember doing anything else. I must have seen Anne in the evenings from time to time, but that job really did occupy me. I got to know the guy who ran the bumper cars, and sometimes took them over for him when he needed a break.

At home the latest was two miniature poodles Mom named Bigi and Pipi. They were great fun for the twins, Alec and Neil, who were five now, and I enjoyed those dogs as well. They were very intelligent, and easy to communicate with.

Near the end of the summer season, about the time when the park closed down I went to an all nighter drink fest at the home of the bumper cars manager, a twenty something with a wife and kids in downtown DC. After the beer we drank whiskey, which produced a tremendous pulsating hangover, the likes of which I had never experienced, and I stayed up all night till the next day, a Sunday I think, my day off. It was time to go to college, and September dawned. I was to be installed in a third floor garret on Greenmount Ave in Baltimore, home of an elderly couple named the Judges, who were eighty years old or more. It was a half mile walk to the campus, and I would bus back home to Bethesda on weekends. I was to share the third floor of the Judges' house with William Kintner, who turned out to be my pro-beat English professor, a late night pot smoking genius. Mr. Kintner did not fraternize with students, and I had no idea what pot was at this time, I guessed from the late night three beer cans and something in his ash tray, that he was smoking something, but it wasn't cigarettes, since there were no butts. It was another couple of years before I got turned on to grass by my brother in law "Goofy," Greg Mc Grath, Natalie's husband to be.

The first thing that I experienced as a Loyola freshman was a beer drinking softball game, and for me the priority was on the beer drinking and not the softball. I don't remember much of that evening, only the beer from the keg was good. I started making friends right away, particularly in my English class, where I met my drinking buddy, John Gillis.

Memorable was our first writing assignment in English. We were asked to read a small book called <u>88 Men and 2 Women</u> about death row inmates, and afterward Dr. Kintner asked us to write an essay on what we would do if we had but twenty-four hours to live. I don't recall what my response was, but I'm sure it would not be different than my normal daily life, with the depression and anxiety that I felt on a regular basis. I got to see a new psychiatrist at the Wyman Drive Public Health hospital that my father once worked when we were on the North Charles St. apartment mentioned earlier. This young doctor was extremely sympathetic, or I was extraordinarily receptive, or both, but I got a lot out of therapy with him, particularly discussing drinking and depression. The only odd thing was that the doctor never really recommended that I stop the drinking. I wonder why not? He had me write out my feelings and thoughts, and I sent them home regularly to my family in the form of letters. I remember feeling homesick and missing them all, and telling them about it.

In English our next event was to read <u>Catcher in the Rye</u>, by J.D. Salinger, the eccentric reclusive author. I felt such a great identification with the main character, Holden Caufield, who was also about seventeen, and quite as neurotic as myself. I realized his feelings that everybody else was "phoney" was based on his faking it himself. At seventeen I felt very much as though I was faking it, now that I was a "young man", and no longer a boy.

Loyola College was a "land grant" college, and therefore had an Army ROTC (Reserve Officer Training Corps). It was time, as I turned eighteen, to decide if I wanted to become an Army Lieutenant while I was going to college. It was also time to register with the Selective Service System, or the Draft. Since joining ROTC guaranteed a 2S deferment from the draft, it seemed like a good idea, and I went for it. I joined the Reserve Army when I turned eighteen in November of '64. I got a smart green uniform, and started training with a .22 target shooting rifle, and marching on the playing fields regularly.

Another activity I took up avidly was playing tennis for three hours at a time after classes, and before dinner. My father gave me an allowance to spend on meals, provided I kept a written record of my expenditures. I ate at a small restaurant around the corner from my Greenmount Ave digs, or occasionally I was invited over to my friend, John Gillis' home for dinner. That usually included wine or beer.

Chemistry was a subject John and I shared, and so we did homework together.

John would bring the "necessary" refreshment, a whole case of beer, up to my room, to help us study better. I actually got a B at the end of the semester, so who knows? My Algebra class was a different story; I couldn't drink beer and still do Algebra. By the end of my first semester I made the Dean's List, and my father and family were thrilled. High school was not moving for me, but this college thing was altogether different, and I loved it.

Going back home on the weekends was all about seeing Anne, going out to eat, double dating with Evie and Brian, playing tennis, and going shooting down at the river with Anne. I remember one day we got together about six AM, and I drove down to the Potomac in the family station wagon. We brought my Winchester .22, and shot at branches, into the water, and I taught her to shoot. She loved it. Later in the day we played tennis, and when she told me she wanted to pour the tennis ball cylinder on me I said OK, and out came water! She soaked me!

I guess old habits die hard, and on one visit back home I went out with some fellows down to the Picolo for a drinking event. I was approached by an older man who put his hands on me, and told me to not be "so tense". That really irritated me, and left me feeling very aggressive. I tore his hands away from me, and moved away. He was obviously gay, and it pissed me off. Once we were really drunk and it was closing time we went out to the parking lot, and I got into a fight with another young man who said he was a wrestler also. I proceeded to head lock him, and then pin him down on the pavement. I realized at that moment that I had the power of life and death over him, and I was already feeling angry from my earlier encounter with the fag, and I wanted to kill him. Something prevented me from doing him any further harm though, and I got back home. I'm not sure who did the driving. It might have been me! Somehow this experience represented a passage for me, the realization that I could *kill*, and it made me contemplate this war that we were becoming involved in, in Viet Nam.

Back at Loyola I attended the required religious events we had at the chapel, and I recall them with fondness, looking back. The administrators (priests) of the college would say the Mass or lead the prayer ceremony with whole student body in attendance. Somehow it was a supernal experience, and I came away from it feeling cleansed. It was around Christmas time, and I remember Dr. Kintner telling me he would be going downtown to listen to the Bach B Minor Mass. I always wondered about that piece of music, and later in life had the chance to hear it. It's not really my favorite Bach piece.

After the holidays I got back to school, and tried out for the wrestling team, and made it. I started eating dinner at the college dining hall, so I could attend practice after classes, around 3:30PM.. I soon lost weight, and tried to wrestle at about 159 pounds. The practices were all consuming, and soon I stopped drinking much, so I could be fit for matches. By the year's end I had won some and lost some, and made a good friend who I went distance running with after practice, coursing through the street lit city streets. After those runs I either did not eat, or went to my neighborhood spot. Swimming was another activity I engaged in regularly, since we had a fine Olympic pool on campus.

1965 had come, and by Spring I got the news that Dad was planning another move, this time to San Francisco, California. My initial reaction was pure glee at the prospect of traveling to the "Golden State", but what about Anne? I would have to leave my girlfriend. We would write to each other, and she would be matriculating into the University of Maryland, where she was admitted. I had served out my probation at Loyola and had maintained my Dean's List status. I was continuing in therapy to the end of the school year, and I was feeling pretty good about myself. I felt proud at having pulled myself out of last year's depression. I applied to another Jesuit university, the University of San Francisco, where I was admitted. They had an ROTC department, and I entered their program.

Dr. Bill Kintner and I had become friends as well as housemates, and I told him about my plans to go to California, he became rather excited by it. He was publisher of a new literary magazine called the" New Directions Reader," a monthly compilation of latest Beat

poetry and short stories. He wanted me to take the first issue to his friend, the Beat Poet, Lawrence Ferlinghetti, at his place, the CityLights book store in North Beach, San Francisco.

I felt truly honored by this introduction, and agreed to take the book to him.

XII

QUINTARA ST. 1965
SAN FRANCISCO

A moving van picked up all our belongings to take to California, and I and my Dad and brother Bob were to travel by car in the old Peugeot Station wagon across country, while Mom, the girls, and the twins flew out. There were powerful farewells and parties prior to our June departure, where the wine poured freely, I think, because I don't remember much about the last days on Battery Lane. Anyway, we were packed in the Peugeot, and took off in early June. I shared the driving, and we were soon into Ohio and the Midwest. There was no air conditioning in cars, generally speaking, so the open window was our air conditioning as we approached the warmer regions. We stopped in motels after about 12-14 hours driving per day, which put us in California in four days. At Donner pass we had an ice chest, and took cubes in our cheeks to stand the 120 degree heat there. In the Nevada desert we also did some shooting with Dad's .25 caliber automatic. Occasionally we'd stop and make a breakfast with our frying pan and cookstove. We ate well and rested well, and in the evenings Dad would give us each a beer or two. I remember arriving in San Francisco, and how truly cold it was. It must have been 50 degrees, and we were in short sleeves!

When we were finally moved into the Quintara St. house I wrote to my psychiatrist in Baltimore, advising him I was well, and no longer needed the Librium. I think I needed to make a formal written closure on my therapy with him. Anyway, it made me feel better.

My next step was to meet with Lawrence Ferlinghetti downtown. I dressed in a sharkskin suit that I bought, and took the bus to North Beach. When I got to the bookstore an employee told me he was with someone up on Columbus in a café, well within walking distance. My apprehension building -what would I say to this famous author?- I arrived at the café and found him in a booth with his friend. It was very much anticlimactic. I greeted him and told him my name, that I was a student of Dr. Kintner, and that I was to give him the New Directions Reader. He thanked me, took the book, and returned to his conversation with the other, basically dismissing me. It was quite a big disappointment, all in all. Maybe I shouldn't have worn the sharkskin suit, I don't know.

I started classes at the University of San Francisco in the Fall, and learned the bus routes in this fascinating city. I also returned to ROTC classes and drills, and slowly learned how to lead a platoon on the field ground. I learned to field strip and reassemble the M1 carbine, the traditional weapon of the last two wars.

XIII

"DAY TRIPPER"

"She took me half the way there...she was a day tripper yeah..." Another number one hit record for the Beatles, played pretty regularly on the radio, along with "You've gotta hide your love away." The LP "Rubber Soul" would also come in '65. The Beatles and the Rolling Stones would both come to America this year, to be guests of Ed Sullivan, on national TV.

I still loved American bands, but after Rubber Soul my standards were raised. John Lennon said that "Ticket to Ride" was the first heavy metal song, and that's not too much of an exaggeration.

I took the government service civil service exam about this time, and qualified for a GS3 position, which I found at Letterman General hospital in the Presidio of San Francisco.

I worked swing shift from three or four to eleven or twelve PM in medical records. I had the position of clerk in a grade equivalent to a buck sergeant, if a serviceman was doing the job. I worked with a black lady named Thelma Blue, and actually dated her, though she was ten years older at least. She was attractive, and was my boss, the supervisor of medical records. There was no hanky panky between us, just dinner at her place, but we had a friendship that was nice.

I wore my hair short now, befitting of an ROTC cadet, and didn't any longer need an Elvis hairdo. I lived with my brother in the basement bedroom of our new house, alongside the garage.

We had our own shower and bath, and I had my neatly refinished secretary desk to study on.

And, study I did a lot of. French literature, including the writings of Montaigne and Voltaire

occupied me, and I became enamored of the thoughts of the Enlightenment. At the same time I took a course in Aristotelian Logic, which helped me with my thinking. The wine parties my father held became apart of my scenario, as I got invited, and the expensive red wine, like Cabernet Sauvignon, went well with my French poetry and philosophy readings. My excursions into the writings of Baudelaire and Francois Villon became all the company I needed. At school I did make one friend, however, and Robert,"Bob" Domergue became my French buddy, with whom I could communicate in French. He was the son of a rich man and French wife, and he had an attractive sister whose name I have forgotten. I understand that later in life Bob became a well to do antiques dealer in San Francisco. We studied French together and later in the year did a teaching apprenticeship with the after school program of the San Francisco school district, grade seven. This after school program is worth mentioning, as the experience of teaching made a strong impression on me. I remember Johnny Greene, who I drove home to the projects after class, where he became a "street urchin" after I dropped him off. One afternoon Johnny punched me hard in the groin, and I hurt for several hours. This little black boy, whose guardians were his mother and an uncle, was headed for trouble, though I never was able to follow up on him.

The We Five hit the music scene in '66 with "You were on my mind", which, if it was not number one on the hit parade, then it was very close. I am not sure if it was '66 or '65, but I first heard them in 1966. What a sound this folk rock group had, with their mix of electric guitars and percussion! I found out that they attended the University of San Francisco, where I think they got together, before they became famous. I never knew them, they must have left by the time I arrived.

Along with Rubber Soul, I now owned their LP as well. I particularly liked their treatment of the Gershwin Porgy and Bess tune, "I've got plenty of nothin'."

In my second semester of my sophomore year I had a U.S. History professor, Father De Glorio, S.J.. He encouraged me to do research into the U.S. Civil war, a project I called "Journey to Accuracy", and for which I spent whole afternoons at the San Francisco Public Library. I had stopped working at the hospital in my civil service job, so had evenings free, and for many of them I worked at the library doing research into the Reconstruction period, which my report was about. My goal was to debunk the Reconstruction era, and I discovered much sadness therein. I must have told it like it was, with its opportunism and abuse of Southern people, because I received an A in that class. I was able to continue with a B average at the University of San Francisco.

I'd like to tell you how I lost my virginity now. I was very lonely one night and I went downtown to an area I knew there were hookers roaming the streets. I came upon one who was a black girl not more than sixteen years old, and went upstairs with her. I remember she was called "Zenobia." We shed some clothing, and before I actually reached a full erection it was over. I came so fast I wondered how sex could be so abrupt. Well, I paid her the ten dollars, and withing two weeks started having painful urinations and a steady drip. I went to the Public Health hospital and discovered I had the "clap" or gonnorhea, and was prescribed penicillin that took care of it. What a denoument!

I bought a 1953 Chrysler Dodge for $35 which ran well. It only needed brakes.

I decided to look for work part time, and found a job through school at the Chevron Service Station 90 Broadway in North Beach, working for Bob Cox, brother to the owner, Barton Cox.

It was a cushy job, for which I was paid the princely Teamster wage of $3.35 per hour, a small fortune at that time. My union membership proved handy when I temporarily dropped out of college in '67. Pumping gas and fixing cars was a great job.

Then I met my brother's school friend, Erik Johnson, a senior like Bob, at Lincoln High School, a basketball star and a class officer. He was very precocious, and became my best friend in the next couple years. Brother Bob was playing football and running track, and doing pretty well academically as well, he encouraged me to start distance running around the Avenues and along Golden Gate park We ran at eleven PM until tired almost each evening for a good while, when it occurred to me try out for the USF football team in the Fall of '66. I was running nonstop for about 45 minutes by then, and felt confident at 175 pounds.

In the summer of '66 I had field training in ROTC at Ft. Bragg, in Marin county, just across the Gold Gate bridge. By this time I had signed my Army contract and started receiving my stipend from the Army Reserves. I was given a sergeants's rank, and was a platoon sergeant. We boarded a drab green Army school bus and were on our way to the hills of Mt. Tamilpias, for a three day weekend training. First we learned about Army procedure of combat planning. Writing up attack plans we learned about the objective and the logistics for it, then shot each other in mock warfare using blanks as ammo. In my first battle I became an actual casualty. One of our boys came alongside me with his M1, firing it at my head level, bursting my ear drum with the sound. Then we had night maneuvers, and became POWs overnight, when we were captured. There was a certain chilling realism to the POW camp: We were placed in lockers, and the outsides were beaten until we were soft in the head from the noise. Then I remember being forced to do seventy-five push-ups at one time. It *was* stressful. By Sunday night we were exhausted, and were riding back home to the campus, turning in our weapons. I hadn't had much sleep, but I felt great! I conveyed to my Dad that the "army life" was for me. The condition in my left ear told me otherwise, and it took about six weeks to heal.

My sister Evelyn had gotten married to her high school sweetheart, John Smeby, who was shipped off to Viet Nam, a member of the Navy's Seabees, to do construction of airfields for the U.S. military. His unit came under attack in, and he became wounded seriously, but not before wheelbarrowing several fellow soldiers to safety, for which he was decorated. He came home in a coma, and for weeks was touch and go, but finally survived his injuries, and after many months could walk again.

I had applied for the football team with Coach Peirsall, wearing an extra sweater to bolster my size. He accepted me, telling me to report for August Summer camp for two weeks of intensive training. We lived in the school dorms, and got up about six AM for breakfast, steaks, eggs, and anything else our hearts could desire. It was opulent, but it burned away after two hours of practice. Then we napped after lunch, until the "double" started about three o'clock, and we worked until dinner time. I did gain weight with the sumptuous meals provided.

The food was awesome, but the practices were difficult, ending with what seemed like interminable running. Finally the football camp came to an end, and school resumed in September. In this my junior year military science took a more serious turn, with studies of battles and military personalities, first aid and tactics designed for the war in Viet Nam.

One day while we were calmly paying attention to our instructor there was a loud bang, and somebody falling into our classroom with his intestines hanging out in front of him. It was extremely realistic, though we discovered it was fake. What a sickening picture he made, enough to give you bad dreams.

San Francisco City College and USF had an agreement to scrimmage each other each year. Brother Bob was now a student and a player there. Bob was a fullback and understudy to the first club fullback, a boy named O.J. Simpson. I played linebacker, and had the chance one time to tackle him on a short play. After about our sixth game in the season I got kicked in the shin while making a tackle at practice. It caused a march fracture (a hairline fracture) in my tibia, and I was out for the season, on crutches. It caused a considerable amount of pain, but I had no choice but to lay back and rest it. It took about fourteen months for it to heal, and it later caused me problems with my lumbar back.

While recuperating I redirected my energy and started playing my electric guitar again. I wrote a song called "Peace, Love, Hate, Fear, Run", about man's search for meaning in a world controlled by fighting in wars. The Army excused me from marching in our assemblies.

I spent a lot of time lying in bed, sitting up with a book or with my guitar. There were many nights with Bob's friend George Kahn and a six pack of beer discussing the meaning of "entropy", or the energy contained in a closed thermodynamic system. Bob and I recorded absurd skits on a little reel to reel tape recorder of my Dad's. One was about a draft inductee who only wanted "to kill, kill, kill", and who therefore was inducted right away. It was slowly out of these meetings that I developed my anti war attitude.

I attended one more semester at USF, starting in January 1967, and I continued in Military science classes and my other degree requirements. Nan started bringing home her boyfriend, Greg Mc Grath, AKA Goofy Mc Grath, who introduced us to marijuana, and later to high quality organic mescaline.

I started to work more at the service station at nights, and to look for a warehouseman job under the Teamsters union. I found that job at the Royal Supply company a supplier to restaurants and bars, cutlery and porcelain et cetera. I continued to work at the service station at night and the warehouse during the day, and soon was bankrolling plenty of money. This is where I met my Irish buddy, Matthew Conlon, who I worked alongside of as a warehouseman. Matt was a hilarious guy about five years my senior, who could spout limericks like nobody's business, and he could drink like the proverbial fish. We used to go out to the Irish pub fairly regularly. He also worked nights at the English fish and chips shop in Haight Ashbury.

He was here on a green card. I shared some of my poems with him, and he liked them. One day, after a particularly heavy night of drinking I wrote a poem on the bathroom door. Shortly after that I was called into the bosses office to explain myself and my rather long poem about each and every member of the office and warehouse staff. I poked fun at small habits and mannerisms of each employee, and I was ready for my walking papers. Suddenly Mr. Hobbs, the owner of the business, said "son, the only broom you should ever have to push is this,,," and he handed me a brand new t-ball jotter from Parker. Ah, the times they were 'a changing.

One evening on a weekend while I was working at the station a young lady and friend came in complaining that her '67 Chevy Chevelle was running poorly and was stalling constantly. I took it in the garage and diagnosed it with a bad fuel pump, by removing the fuel line and pumping it. The next day was a Saturday, and I was fortunately able to get a fuel pump from an auto supplier, and replaced it. That Friday night we went out with Darlene and her friend. Tommy, my coworker at the station, drove his Volkswagen, and before we took them to their motel room we had a few beers somewhere and talked. They next day they picked up their car, and Darlene invited me to come to her home in Sacramento. Darlene was this model-like figure standing 5 ft. 8 inches tall, and one of the most beautiful blondes I ever met. On Sunday I drove to Sacramento to her garden apartment with swimming pool, and we made love, and sat by the pool afterwards. She was a year older than I, twenty-two, and had been abused by her GI ex-husband, a year or so earlier. With us it was a classic case of love at first sight, and I started to visit her on weekends. One night I invited her to my downstairs bedroom at home, where she stayed the night with me in my single bed. My Dad found out, and was rude to her, asking her to leave, and giving me notice that I had to move out and find my own place. There was a neighbor down the street who was looking for a place and a roommate to share expenses. Rodger had just been discharged from the Air Force, and I found him to be a really great guy, so we started looking for, and found a two bedroom apartment in Pacific Heights. It wasn't cheap, but it was a high rent district, so we liked it. It had a communal kitchen upstairs that came in handy.

I used to go make deposits at a local bank near Royal Supply downtown, and met a teller, who seemed interested in me. We went out to dinner one week night and came back home to my place. She smoked pot like I did, so we soon got into bed with a joint. I remember hallucinating Disney cartoon characters on my wall after we made love. It was a magical evening, but because of Darlene it was not repeated. She was a sweet chick, but it was the sixties, and anything went.

My lumbar back started to hurt, and especially when I braked in my old Dodge, whose brakes were always hard to press. The heavy lifting at the warehouse with handcarts was causing me to feel my low back after work. I didn't think much of it at first, and it would fade altogether some times. It seemed like there was a connection between my broken leg and my lower back; Like the weakness in the leg had me lifting off balance.

Erik Johnson had gone off to U.C. Berkeley after high school on a basketball scholarship, and he had pledged the Sigma Phi fraternity, which I would soon pledge also.

We had been seeing each other off and on for the past two years, and in the summer we traveled to Northern California up to go river rafting on the American river. We bound two truck inner tubes together and started down the river with a case of beer, after first saturating ourselves a bit on dry ground. It was a warm day, and the alcohol fast took its toll on me. About halfway through the course our makeshift raft broke apart leaving me with my tube and him with his.

The next thing I remember was floating face down in the river in a calm spot with a terrible pain in the head. I was bleeding from my skull, and realized I must have collided with a rock in the river going down a rapid without my tube, headfirst. Lucky to be alive, I came out of the river near our destination, and called it a day, with some first aid. I was very numb from all the beer I drank.

The so called "Summer of Love" 1967 was a summer when hippies from everywhere around the United States descended upon San Francisco, and one of them was our old band mate, Eddie Roche. Eddie brought his guitar and Vibrolux Fender amp with him, and found a job south of San Francisco in Pacifica, at a horse rent stables, where he cleaned the stables and fed the horses, for room and board, and a small wage. He also found gigs playing and singing in some bars in town. He had discovered Bob Dylan, and learned a few of his songs. He turned me on to Bob Dylan, and what a turn on it was. I learned to play accompaniment to "Sad Eyed lady of the the Lowlands," "I want You" and "Just Like a Woman", as well as "Lila", an original. Ed was into writing songs now, and when we were not riding "Socks" and "Spike" along the beach we were in the bunk house plunking out tunes, and rolling joints.

Erik was encouraging me to come over to UC Berkeley, and join his fraternity. He told me that the Dean of admissions was a Sigma Phi alumnus, and could pull strings if necessary to insure my admission. I made application, and submitted transcripts from the two colleges, and despite a B average, it was agreed I could be accepted on probation. In the meantime I spent many a happy weekend with Darlene, but sometime in the Fall of '67 she told me she did not want to see me anymore. I think she wanted a more permanent commitment from me, and we parted ways. I started to write to Anne again, and felt I really needed her. She had had a boyfriend who got her pregnant, and she had had an abortion. We corresponded until September of '68, when we finally met up again.

I started at Berkeley in February '68, and took a weightlifting course for the physical education requirement. I quickly had injured my lumbar back, and had to see a doctor at the university, as well as stop taking the course. I was called by the ROTC department for a physical at the Presidio base in San Francisco. I was examined by an Army doctor, and there was the possibility of a slipped disc. I was honorably discharged from the Reserves, but now I was 1A in my draft status.

I took up residence at the Sigma Phi fraternity house after pledging, and started partying seriously, while continuing the use of pot. I commuted to San Francisco to my part time job at the service station. I was making as much money part time as a lot of people working lower wage full time jobs. I would soon experience a low wage part time job, when my hair got longer and Barton Cox didn't approve, in late '68, and fired me. He didn't like the change.

I had traded my Dodge to Erik for his Honda 305 Scrambler, so my travels over to the city were made on motorcycle. Many a happy hour I spent riding the Honda between Berkeley and San Francisco. Some of my first courses at Berkeley included Genetics and Paleontology, and something called the U.S. Federal System. I have a fond memory of Genetics, as it was taught by Linus Pauling, the famous scientist. I got an A in that course, miraculously. Paleontology so impressed me that I discussed careers with the department head, who unfortunately told me that the likelihood of jobs out in the field were slim. He said that a typical graduate got a job as museum curator. Yuck! Cross that one out.

"Coffee Cat". That's what I called the character of my play that I wrote in spasms, in between coming down from my pot high. Coffee always brought me down, and so I kept a large instant coffee supply in the frat house kitchen. When I was twelve my scoutmaster,

Joe Palermo, turned me on to coffee with milk and sugar, trying to get me awake and on the bus with him on our trip to summer camp. I recall being in a deep sleep while being marched to the bus stop, and then that coffee hit me. It tasted good. When it went down in my stomach it was like I'd been injected by a needle, the rush of wakefullness, awareness, was so great. It was my first turn on to drugs, introduced by a community leader! It's no wonder I wanted to write a short play about a cat who loved coffee, and in fact I drank it nonstop while I was studying.

By the time summer came I was missing Anne, and wanted to plan a trip back East to see her. That summer was quiet, and filled with service station work and classes. A visitor to our fraternity house who shared the name of my manager, was Bob Cox, from Harvard. He roomed above me, and we became good friends, and it was his suggestion that we take a Mustang back East that a friend of his had left. So, come summer's end we had but to put gas in this nice car, and we were on our way East to deliver it. We slept out in the open at night, and one night late we stopped in the dark at this very large lawn, with some nondescript buildings back a ways from the road. In the morning we awoke to find a sign with State Mental Hospital on it. Oh well. Another night in the rain we found a train yard with some broken down cars on it. We tried to sleep in the railway car, but the rain found its way into it, and we were forced to sleep in the car, without much room. On the fourth day we arrived in Bethesda, and I was reunited with my Anne. We were able to stay with my sister Evie and her husband, John Smeby.

Better late than never, Anne and I made love for the first time in their upstairs bedroom, with my brother Bob staying over with his girlfriend, my sister Evie's close friend, Connie. I don't recall what Bob was doing back East at that time, but he was. When we went back to

Anne's home her mother intuited that something was up since she didn't come home last night, and we announced our plan to get married, and to leave for California, back to Berkeley.

My new friend, Bob Cox, was still with us, and I requested he be best man, with my uncle, Father

Tony Buchness, presiding over the marriage at Our Lady of Lourdes Church in Bethesda. I borrowed a suit from my brother in law, John Smeby. We had a pleasant small wedding with Anne's mother in attendance (her father refused in protest). Anne and I flew from Dulles International Airport a short while later, and we arrived in San Francisco with the task of informing my fraternity brothers that I would no longer be one, as I was a married man now. Erik was very disappointed at my short duration fraternity pledge, and fronted me a kilo of grass for my wedding gift, as he was now a dealer, making lots of money. I would sell the pot and return to him the wholesale cost. It was a nice gift.

We found an apartment on Grove St. right away, I returned to school, and Anne took a job at Berkeley Fabrics, a business she had some familiarity with from her college course in Fashion Design. I found a '62 Chevy Corvair with a banged up front, whose hood I was able to chain down with a lock. We set up house in our one bedroom apartment, and I grew my hair long, and lost my service station job as the result, and slowly started looking for some place to work in Berkeley. I took a job on campus as a clerk for Phi Beta Kappa for several hours a week.

It was on Grove St. I experienced a couple of bad trips. One night we had some particularly strong weed, or hashish maybe, when the pan with kipper snacks turned into snakes, and sent me running up the street until I was out of breath. I came back home and was settled down some, and no longer hallucinating. Another time I had gotten some bella donna from my next door neighbor, Steve. I was cold and I thought I was about to die, and just waited for the ill effects to subside, which they did several hours later. I decided to lay off drugs for a while. I had turned Anne on, too, by the way, and she enjoyed getting high on grass.

It was when we were first married that I bought albums by Led Zeppelin and Jimi Hendrix, and played them whenever I got a break from studying. It was about this time that I found a jamming/smoking partner in a Philippino guy in the neighborhood, who played the blues, and taught me a lot of riffs on the guitar. I also took lessons from another guitarist,

Tim Kalhatsu, who played with the Charlie Musselwhite Blues Band. They lived for a while in town, and played the local night spots. My blues chops were coming along fine when my jamming partner, whose name escapes now, took me to an all black party in San Francisco.

I put my amp on stage, and was climbing up when the band leader kicked my amp nearly off the stage, and told me without saying it, that I was not welcome there. Embarrassed, in my bell bottoms we left, Anne and I, and went back to Berkeley, feeling quite bruised by this act of reverse racism.

On the weekends Anne and I used to go over to visit Eddie in Pacifica, share a bottle of wine, of course smoke, and make music. My parents were still living on Quintara, and we'd on occasion visit them. My father was about to invoke the "three year rule", it being 1968, and this time he had his sights set on Denver, Colorado, where he would help administer the building of Public Health and Veterans hospitals in the Western states. My father and I had drifted so far apart during the San Francisco period that I never did learn what he was doing job wise. I only knew that he worked out of the Federal building downtown. So my family would go with Bobby and the twins to live in a new and strange city. Bob got a football scholarship to the University of Colorado, and took up Sociology. Sister Natalie got married to Goofy Mc Grath, and stayed on in San Francisco in a kind of commune house in the Mission district. My parents gave Anne and me a going away/wedding gift of enough money to purchase a strereo, for which we were very grateful. Evie had moved back to Bethesda with John Smeby and their new daughter, Lori. They would be together only for a short while longer, as John's post traumatic stress disorder was causing him to beat up on her, and eventually caused their breakup.

Well, it was inevitable the Selective Service would finally catch up to me, and my induction notice was received some time in the Spring of '69. I was instructed to report to the Oakland Induction center for evaluation. I was totally unprepared for this, and had heard many stories of boys who had wiggled out of the draft one way or another. One way was to leave the United States for Canada. Another way was to take LSD going into the examination. One novel method I heard about had actually occurred: a guy wore wader boots filled with yellow paint, and was playing his saxophone when he arrived. Naturally he was ordered to take the waders off, and so all over the induction center floor did flow the bright yellow paint. I understand he was not accepted for military service. Perhaps he was arrested?

Anyway, I was asked to bend over a touch my toes, which I couldn't actually do for the pain I had regularly in my lumbar spine. About a month later I received a "4F" draft classification in the mail. I was enthralled, saved by my bad back. I was indeed lucky.

This was my last year in school, so I was taking classes that interested me, like Deviant Sociology and a ground floor seminar on Marxism, which I had to drop as it was a graduate course, and was totally incomprehensible to me. I opted instead for Cultural Geography, which was an exploration of the thoughts of Alexander Von Humboldt, on the nature of how humans influence geography. At about this time there was an awful lot of antiwar activity on the campus, and I kept up with it, along with my little job at the Laundromat /dry cleaners. There were marches around Berkeley, which Anne and I joined to protest the conduct of the war. One day there was some serious activity for which the Alameda county sheriffs were brought in. I know, because when I tried to see over the gathered crowd I got a billy club jabbed into my Adam's apple, robbing my of speech for about a day or more. Back then there were no ways to redress these kinds of wrongs. Police brutality was a common occurrence. People were even killed, like the unfortunate young man shot by a deputy, while he was on the roof from which someone had been hurling bricks down on the police. The young man was innocent, but the police claimed they were defending themselves

I ran into Sam Cole while I was looking both for a job and a new dwelling. He was a young lawyer from Berkeley who had a few houses for rent, that also needed a maintenance man, and I was in need of that job. I was glad to learn about houses and their maintenance, and to get a place of my own to look after was a real plus. Sam was a liberal and a great employer it turned out, he became a good friend and benefactor. We moved into the Fulton St. house near Ashby with Dan Bowles and Marty Mc Grath, Greg's older brother. Dan had been living with Steve Kreiger on Grove St. On the houses I had the assistance of Country Joe Mac Donald's father, who knew everything about fixing houses. Country Joe and the Fish was a very popular Hippie rock band from Berkeley, who had a recording contract with a major label.

They came to national attention with their hit single about Viet Nam, which had the refrain "we're all gonna die" in it. I think they were a featured act at Woodstock.

Anne and my new roommates were an ex-Marine Corps Sergeant, Marty McGrath who was also a student, and whose main activity seemed to be smoking dope in large quantity and reading hip books. He was an interesting strange stray cat. Dan Bowles was from Van Nuys, California, and was an All American gymnast who specialized in the high bar. He was an extremely good humored young man, who attended Cal on a sports scholarship. The four of us got along wonderfully, and Anne and my rent was paid by my odd jobs on the houses Sam owned. It was an ideal arrangement for a young couple and students.

We had a good time living on Fulton St. in the two story four bedroom house, and would take trips over to Marin County where my parents owned a cabin in Bolinas, down near the ocean. It was in Bolinas one weekend that we experienced organic mescaline for the first time. Except for having to vomit in the first hour of the trip it was lovely and filled with beautiful hallucinations of nature. We sat on the beach and watched the ocean for several hours, still as the still weather that surrounded us. Then we went back to Berkeley with a fresh mind and new awarenesses. The trip lasted about sixteen hours.

In the Spring of '69 I began studying Constitutional Law, which went by the name "Legal Institutions," and I found something that really interested me. Case analysis absorbed me totally, and especially the topics of civil liberties in the first and second amendments. The course was taught by Donald Aiken, an apparent important legal light of the time. He was a very exciting teacher whose lectures always held my interest. I contemplated going to law school, but never followed through on it. I had an equally engaging interest in music, and I took a course in contemporary music, following a course in Music theory. On Fulton St. I learned my first piece of classical guitar, a prelude in c minor by Bach. It was difficult, but worth the effort when I accomplished it. I also became interested in jazz, and subscribed for the first time to Downbeat magazine. Marty Mc Grath helped me in this interest, as he had many recordings of jazz and Bossa Nova in his record collection. During one of our weekends in Bolinas thieves broke in, or rather, walked in (since we never kept our place locked) and stole most of my record collection.

That was quite a blow, but the records were the only objects taken, so we were lucky in that sense.

The academic year of 1969 was passing with the memory of the loss of Robert Kennedy and Martin Luther King the previous year. Our visits to see Eddie Roche were fewer since we started going to Bolinas, but once about this time we went over to the city, and dropped acid for the first time. I remember Eddie taking us to the apartment previously rented by Jorma Kakunin of the Jefferson Airplane, their bassist. He was looking around for an apartment, and we spent the first few hours of our trip there, just vegetating. Anne became anxious and seemed to be having a bad trip, and needed talking down. I was fine with it, however, and felt LSD was very exciting in a weird sort of way. By the next day we were straight again, and Anne was alright, but didn't want to take acid again. I felt the same way, finally, and did not take it again.

This was also the time following the Charles Manson murders, which left a bad taste in the mouths of most hippies, since his was considered a hippie commune of sorts.

I came out of my contemporary music course with only a C minus; apparently my comprehension of contemporary classical music was, and still is, kind of limited. I still find most of it boring, with few exceptions. In the winter quarter of 1970 I took courses in Renaissance history and Modern Social Movements, a funny juxtaposition of old and new, but fascinating. I studied about the history of labor unions in the United States. What a violent history it was!

In my final quarter, Spring 1970, I took courses in Nature, Cultural Relations (Geography), U.S. History 1787-1845, and Social Psychology, Comparative Analysis. The courses I found were intensely interesting, but then Governor, Ronald Reagan, decided to close down the campus about halfway through it. The campus was regularly filled with tear gas during that quarter, and it became impossible to hold classes. We all received "Pass/Fail" grades that quarter, and I graduated in June, 1970, without any fanfare or celebration. What a disappointing end to a college career!

XIV

1970

The end of the school year saw a calm on campus, and a diminishment of antiwar activity. I was plain tired of school and the war, and I was ready to try new things. I went to downtown Oakland to answer a cab driver ad, after taking a test for juvenile services and not hearing from the state afterwards. My cab driving experience was a catastrophe. The job was with a black owner, who seemed less than enthusiastic about me, a hippy. I drove all day, and by the days' end received a wage of about two and half dollars. He didn't have to fire me, I quit willingly. It was another case of reverse racism, but I took it in stride. African Americans had been through a lot lately.

I ran into John Robin, a guitarist who enjoyed rock a' billy music as well as country western, one of my latest flames. I had become obsessed through Merle Haggard with Jimmy Rodgers. I learned a few of his songs to sing and strum, along with some Hank Williams numbers, like the "Lovesick Blues," and others like Johnny Cash's. We practiced in our new house on Rose St., rented the summer of '70. Soon we were playing with a country band on Mission St. in San Francisco that summer. The band members called us the "Mission St. Miracles". It was composed of a pedal steel player, a bass player and drummer, so with me singing and playing rythmn guitar and John playing lead guitar we had a pretty good sound for a pick up band. Of course, we only knew about ten songs, so we didn't continue. We did keep practicing on Rose St. drinking a quart of beer at the same time, and not so much pot, as it interfered with our learning new things.

I went back to the Cox management company and tried to find a job running one of their parking garages. I started swing shift at the Japanese Cultural Center, and in very short time learned an appropriate bow to customers coming in and going. The pay was union scale, and therefore hard to turn down. Commuting to SF was not so bad. Our rent was high, and we grew a garden to grow vegetables. We had two cats, a grown gold Lab named Chloe, and later her five puppies, when she mated with an Irish setter. This produced beautiful pups with longish hair.

I soon got transferred to a better job, at the Franciscan Restaurant, Bayside, where it was sunny most days. I collected tickets and fees while I gazed at the island of Alcatraz across about a mile of water. This was a job that allowed me to get high on pot while I sketched and wrote poetry. At that point in my life I got high a lot, in fact, I stayed high most of the time, and life was good. I never got interested in other drugs, like some people with heroin and soft drugs in the form of pills. I was very much influenced by the Zen commune that we lived next door to on Fulton St. I spent time with them meditating without drugs, and practicing basic yoga asanas. They were a good influence on me, and like most hippies I experienced pot and the hallucigens, but left the bad stuff alone. I am very glad of that.

1971 found me buying a VW Beetle, a 69' I think it was, but in good shape, beige and nice to look at. I sold the Corvair for about $75, which was good, since I only paid about two hundred for it. Now I had a car that I could drive to Denver to visit my folks with. So, at the end of winter we drove across the Rockies into a late winter blizzard on the other side, which was scarey. We pulled over until it stopped snowing the next day, having to shovel our car out. The highway was pretty covered with snow, but the bug seemed to manage it, and we reached Denver in one piece. When we got there we discovered that the family was planning another move in summer, back to Catonsville..

We had pleasant visit with my parents, Bob and the twins, and did a good deal of drinking, though I didn't let on that drink for me had become an adjunct to good pot. My mother at that time had it as a steady diet, however. Her drinking went mostly unnoticed. One of the nice outcomes from this visit was that Chloe mated with an Irish Setter. I know who she mated with because after coitus they needed to be separated; he was stuck way up inside of her! It took about a half hour for them to separate!

By the time we returned to Berkeley a week or two later, I had decided that we should also move back East to be with Grand Doc. He was suffering from lymphoma and at 71 years of age it was sad that he was pronounced terminally ill. I wanted to find a bluegrass influenced band to play with, possibly in the Virginia area, or around Baltimore. So we packed up all our belongings and put them (including my upright piano) in a U Haul van with a tow hitch on the rear for the VW.. We took our small savings and left jobs and people behind (I was doing it again!). We slept in the van on our double bed, with the dog and the puppies in the cab, on the wide seat. It was a pleasant journey, except for when some of the pups got car sick and vomited all over the seat. They soon got used to it, however, and we moved on. We arrived on Newburg Ave. exhausted at about five AM one morning, only to find that Grand Doc had passed on a little while ago. It was a depressing homecoming with my Dad less than welcoming, but we were soon moved into the "Big House," where we stayed for several months. That Fall, 1971, my brother, Bob, and I sought jobs in construction with Peters and Taylor roofers, hot tar flat top roof construction. We must have worked a month or two, until the cold weather prevented us from continuing. After that it was men's fashions at the Mongomery Wards in Westview shopping center for me, and the Montgomery County Police for Bob. Then I was approached by my gay cousin, Gregory, with an offer of a job with him, working for Leo Amster in the formal wear shop of the same name. He was opening another branch in Gen Burnie, and would I like to be its first manager? A manager position sounded too good to be true, and as it turned out was just that. I was alone in a store space renting tuxedos in a quiet section of a Glen Burnie shopping center. Too quiet. I developed a routine of getting high, and listening to tapes on my Panasonic tape and radio player. After a month or two of that I was burned out on the down time. I think "Uncle Leo" may have caught on to the back room smoking one day, and maybe smell the marijuana. In any case he explained to me that I was a bad fit for the job and fired me. I immediately found a job at the Lafayette radio in the same shopping center, the manager was a gay who had something of a crush on me, which made me feel quite uncomfortable. I got tired of being treated differently from other employees and expressed it by throwing the large trash bin down the center of the store one day. It got me fired, but I was leaving anyway.

Anne and I found a first floor on Edmondson Ave. in Hunting Ridge, just near the Catonsville line in Baltimore city. We rented the nice flat in an older converted flagstone large home. It had a basement, and it was very comfortable. I found a job with the U.S. Census Bureau, working on what was called President Nixon's urban crime survey. I conducted interviews with households and businesses for about three months, when the survey wound down. It was an interesting job finding out about real experiences of crime, and I was sad to leave it. I found a job selling hifi next on Lombard St. down the street from my father's medical practice he'd inherited from his father and his uncle Anthony. I remember it was number 12 East Lombard St., and was eventually sold to the Playboy Club when Dad wanted to retire for a while, maybe to grieve the loss of his father. So I went to work for Henry O. Berman Electronics, in the stereo-hifi room. Earlier in the year I had taken the State of Maryland professional careers test, and would be notified if jobs became available.

Selling stereo goods was not so financially rewarding as might have been possible if old Mr. Berman did some advertising, which he refused to do, although he was marketing quite high end equipment like Marantz, Mac Intosh and Pioneer. I worked with two fellows my own age, named Jim Kelly and Ric Puller. Kelly was a minor rock star who in 1965 had a number two or three single behind the Beatles number one hit, "Ticket to Ride". His song was called "Throw Stones", but it never went anywhere beyond Baltimore. Ric Puller was an actor with a degree in Drama. Both of these coworkers had things for me to do with them. Jim Kelly wanted to form a band with me, and he had a remarkably pretty voice, so I took up with him and learned his songs, all good FM singles like Bread's big hit, "Sweet Surrender".

Ric Puller wanted me to act in a modern play, and play the lead role, at the "Corner Theater" on North Howard St. He gave me the script, and introduced me to the young director. The director felt I was right for the role, and told me to rehearse it. Unfortunately, there were complications preventing me concerning my next employment. The Jim Kelly band practiced around Dundalk, and we got gigs, like weddings and parties in big places. Jim could really sing, but when I was offered the state job, the band broke up.

I was called into an interview for the Division of Parole and Probation with a panel of about eight gentlemen, and I guess I said the right things, so I got offered a job working for the State, but funded by the Federal government, the Y3 Impact Project. This was a specially picked team of twenty that was put together to intensively supervise mainly parolees who were convicted of major, or "impact" crimes, murder, rape, aggravated assault, armed robbery, and large drug offenses. The recidivism rate was highest with this group, and supervision was a challenge.

The "Impact Project" was housed at 2104 N.Charles St. in Charles Village, not far from the Maryland Institute of Art. There was a sandwich shop down the street a few doors, that featured organic, whole and vegetarian foods. Our jobs were primarily on the road, "in the field" as we referred to it, and we were paid per diem mileage, driving our private cars. Immediately I got a car loan to buy my first new car, a 1973 VW Beetle convertible, black top, orange body, a real cute car.

Our first task was to complete the Parole and Probation Academy, and to visit the Md. Correctional Training Center, and stay with the inmates, yes, locked up inside with the inmates. It was a three day experiment to give us a sense of verisimilitude, or empathy with our clients. I was twenty six years old, and our clients were between 18 and 26 years old. So, they were very close in age. They could not have been farther apart in background, though, from our solidly middle class families from the suburbs.

Our stay in MCTC Hagerstown was a rather solitary experience, for we stayed in a 4ft.X10ft. cell. I immediately did pushups and situps to distract myself from its claustrophobia. We were allowed out where there was a loud television up in a corner. The noise was deafening. The community was relaxed and nice enough, just like a bunch of kids pulled out of their home environments of street corners and playing fields.

We agents finished up our stay by getting steaming drunk on beer and playing guitars and singing out on the grassy lawns of the Warden's house where we stayed the last night. We returned to Baltimore severely hung over, but I suppose we were ready to set up office and begin seeing the clients who reported for the first time following their incarceration. After that one contact in the office we would see them weekly on their own turf in the city, or on their jobs.

We were each assigned twenty parolees and a few probationers from the circuit court that fit our profile. Our Field supervisor was Fred Gearhardt, a former prisoner of war of the Nazis, and he always seemed a bit tense, but he had a good sense of humor. And, he didn't sit around all day telling war stories. My first partner was Donald Steil, a smooth operator a few years senior and not new to the Agency. He soon became a supervisor, and I got another partner, Jim Hammer, and ex Catholic priest, about thirty five.

One of the first times we signed out into the field we ended up at Don Steil's house with another senior agent named Jerry Levy, who sat us down to play poker. I opted out for picking around on Don's guitar. Donald was interested in the blues and folk music, and had plenty of good records. We talked a lot about Blues and Country stars we both knew.

After the first year seeing those clients became smoother, and I felt I could relax more, until one day knocking on a client's door I get an answer from within that sounded distressed. As he opened the door he stayed behind it as it slowly moved open. In his right hand he held a revolver pointed at the door, with me on the other side of it. He came to admit the reason he was armed thus: he was afraid of heroin users/dealers he had dealings with. I could see the fear in him, and didn't confiscate the weapon, but he found his way back to prison, where he was probably safer than on the street. I had him "retaken" as the expression went, for violating the parole rule against possession of dangerous or deadly weapons.

My starting pay as a Parole Agent was $8500 a year, which at the time,1973, was a bundle. I started buying records by the armful, and started playing my guitar. At this time I still saw my gay cousin, Greg, and one night we got together, got high and a little drunk too.

We discussed openly having a sexual experience, but I got cold feet, and found I was unable to commit to it. He was okay about that. I still felt a love for my cousin, who died sadly of AIDS in the late eighties. He always wanted to write a story about a boy and his little dog, but the dog was actually a little joint that he kept with him, having many adventures with. I guess he never got around to it

As I worked my Parole and Probation job I had the constant reminder of an incarceration I suffered only seven years earlier, in San Francisco City Prison, when I was just nineteen. One night I was out alone hopping bars, when I went into one in the Avenues, close to the beach. I chanced to meet a brunette maybe ten years older than I, and had a drink or two with her. I think in my immature (drunk) frame of mind I was falling in love with her. She was pretty and a hippy, something new to me at that time. She invited me up to her apartment in the vicinity, and we listened to records, Bob Dylan included. We made love in her small bed, and stayed up until late. This was 1966, and I hadn't been introduced yet to pot, so we only drank some wine she had. I left late and told her I'd see her again. After that I day dreamed about this woman constantly.

I was afraid to go over to her place sober, she was only my second sexual experience in my life, and I felt embarrassed. I thought she wouldn't want to see me again for some reason. So, the next time I got together with Erik Johnson to drink ourselves stupid, we ventured into her direction. First we chugged two whole fifths of red wine, and maybe some beer too. I was blind drunk, but I had the courage to go visit her then. I went up the stairwell, and stumbled into her place, after first encountering a man she was with. I think I was so drunk I expressed a jealousy against the man, maybe in a threatening manner also. I left Erik down in his car waiting for me to invite him up. I never returned to Erik. The cops were called and a complaint of trespassing was made. Two young police handcuffed me and took me out of the apartment. Their plan was to take me home and drop me off at a home where I was welcome.

They took me to the house, and I, for some mad reason didn't want my mother to see me in that condition. I became violent and threatened the cops if they tried to take me into the house.

I was completely irrational because of the wine. They put me back in car and hauled me off to San Francisco City Prison, where I was booked for public drunkenness and locked up. I don't remember much after that. I think I blacked out on the floor of my cell. This all might have been different if my Dad was in town, but he wasn't. He was traveling in some western state. Mom contacted her brother, my uncle Albert, who I met with the following morning, and he had gone my small bail. Uncle Al was very understanding, and I was in a terrible hang over, and my head hurt, because I had apparently been banging my head on the floor. About two weeks later I had a trial, to which I pled guilty to drunkenness, and was fined $12.50. The day after my jailing the two officers came around the house to make sure I was alright. I thought that was very special; they were good cops. I never saw the girl again.

XV

1975, DANIEL ALLEN, AND BANDS

In 1974 Anne became pregnant with my first child, Daniel Allen. Anne had found a decent job working in the pharmacy of Mercy Hospital in downtown Baltimore. She was considered a pharmacy Tech, and made a good salary. I had been with the Parole and Probation Agency for over a year now, and had passed through my probationary period. Things were going pretty well, and I had found some guys to play music with: Gary Slavinsky, bass, Bob Armstrong, piano, and Phil Townes, drums. We called ourselves "Vertebrae," and started learning cover tunes from the top 40. We practiced in my basement, after it was soundproofed with egg cartons.

One of the first agendas we had as a band was to buy identical uniforms of wide collars and bell bottoms slacks. We all went shopping together at the Gap, or something like it, and picked up the suits. I was told to spend on uniforms and on LP records by my tax accountant William Kamerow, who was affectionately known by Tom Trimble of my office, as "the Shade."

I came to know Bill as my uncle Bill, for all the money he got me back at tax time. He suggested I purchase between $30 and $50 a month in records as materials used in my "music service", which was certainly easy for me to do, as I loved buying new music each month. $30 in 1974 was the value of $180 in today's money! Uncle Bill's instructions also included all my hifi and band music equipment, so I bought a new Gibson Les Paul in a cherry sunburst finish, and a Fender Twin reverb amp with Electrovoice speakers. Nothing was too good for this enterprise, and couldn't be used to eliminate income taxes. This was free enterprise.

One of Vertebrae's first gigs was at a dance club called the Hollywood Palace outside of Catonsville on Rt. 40. It was a big place with a big stage, and featured name acts like Rory Gallagher and Robert Palmer. We were there to open for Sinbad, a top 40 group that was popular in and around Baltimore. They liked us, and offered us a chance to tour with them.

Alas, we were all part time and couldn't make that commitment. Our first night out in the big time was a disaster. Gary stepped off the five foot high stage backwards, and fortunately fell in such a way as not to hurt himself. I sang "Mandy" by Barry Manilow, and my voice squeaked.

Bob Armstrong acquitted himself well and saved the night for us with his rendition of "Midnight Rider" by Greg Allman. Our version of "Lucy in the Sky with Diamonds" in

reggae beat was one of my favorites. We all learned a lot from the experience of playing the Hollywood Palace.

Back on the home front I was training with my wife in Lamaze breathing exercises, and all that went with that. It was now 1975, and my immediate Supervisor sold me his '67 Chevrolet Impala for some minimum amount of money, so I got a well worn, but well cared for car. It had a 327 engine, and could really pick up when it had to. Selling me that car was a nice gesture by Rabe Benbennick. I drove the Chevy on my job, and gave the new VW to Anne. We had fun with the Impala when we took it to the Westview Drive in to see the latest films. The big wide front seat whose back reclined was de luxe. I don't know how many more years that Drive in operated, but it sure was fun while it lasted.

One cold morning in the winter of '75 I noticed that the windows of the house next door, a very nice house, were broken out and glass was all over. I called the police and was greeted by a young officer about my age who wanted to go inside and investigate. The home had been rented by Gypsies, judging from their comings and goings and guests. I shared badges with the officer, and he handed me his sidearm, saying "here, hold this while I climb in the window." I held his pistol while he managed to get inside the house and open the front door. Inside we found the whole place cleaned out of furniture and goods- they had left in a hurry. There were Sears receipts for credit of stunning amounts. The place was empty, and my poor landlord, who also owned this house, had a lot of repairs to make.

On July 15,1975 I was twenty eight years old, Anne, twenty seven, and that evening her water broke. By 3:15 AM on the sixteenth I had helped with the birth of my son, Daniel Allen, and of course, I felt ecstatic. I took the day off, went home to visit with Gary, and did some drinking with him. We took Danny home the next day, with all okay. We started thinking about buying a home, and found an end house of a row house development on Random Rd. in South Chapelgate, within the city limits. The house was on a hill, and its basement was inside that hill, so it was a good rehearsal space for the band. We were able to assume a veteran's mortgage at a low interest rate, and soon we were moving to Random Rd. with the new little boy.

Dad was disillusioned with the industrial medical practice on Lombard St., and he put his antennae out for a new job. He was now retired from the Public Health Service, and learned of a vacancy of a Health Officer on Maryland's Eastern shore. He sold his building for about $100,000 to Hugh Hefner and the Playboy Club. He sold Grand doc's "Big House" and property to a local doctor, and moved to a 60 acre farm in Allen, Maryland, just south of Salisbury, Md.. They moved in with the twins, Alec and Neil, and set up home in an old farm house in need of some refurbishment.

In its third year the Impact Project was winding down, and preliminary findings pointed to the overall conclusion that intensive supervision reduced recidivism of ex-offenders.

I had a young black man named Michael Wilkes who had murdered someone, and was now out on parole under intensive supervision, (as were all our clients.) This twenty year old was convicted as a juvenile, and he had a good attitude toward supervision, and sincerely appreciated my help with finding him a job program and so forth. He was my poster child, a success for the Impact Project. Another white boy, Bobby Gold, was a convicted drug dealer, who was maimed in jail when an enemy dropped, from a height, a full bucket on his head, causing him brain damage of some sort. He was for the most part alright, though he had a severe scar across his brow where the bucket had cut him. He had "burned" some fellows on a drug deal he had conducted before his incarceration. He told me he had enemies on the outside, and one day showed me two .38 caliber cartridges he received from one of them who had visited him the previous day. Several days later at 6AM I received a call from Bobby's mother who cried "Bobby's dead" repeatedly.

That was a very distressing wake up. Bobby was found in the river near his home, apparently drowned, but also with a head wound, like from a baseball bat. His death was suspicious, and never solved. I felt like I had lost a brother, Bobby was a good kid who was trying to do the right thing. I grieved his loss for several months. Sometime in 1976 the Impact Project concluded and I was reassigned to a special caseload downtown on Calvert St., working for the Supreme Bench, the main criminal court. My position was picked up by the State of Maryland, so I had made it into State Service.

I started in a basement office at 12 N. Calvert St. and was assigned to a woman supervisor named Diane Fielding. No more small caseload, I then received around one hundred cases for collection of court fees and restitution and fines. I had reached the bottom, and chased around town in the inner city after probationers owing monies, all with deadlines. Many of these cases were from violation of child support orders. So, now I had become a Probation Officer/ Collections Agent. I was not happy, and started having psychological difficulties dealing with something I had never experienced, to wit, a female boss. I went to an Hispanic psychiatrist recommended to me by former coworker, Jerry Levy. I was told I was suffering from "castration anxiety", implying that I needed to get a male supervisor. So, here I was in an office located one block off of Baltimore's notorious "Block", a sex trade district of Baltimore

St., lined with sex shops and night clubs with topless dancers, and I was being bossed by a strict woman supervisor.

What a juxtaposition! One consolation of my new job was that I had the opportunity to eat lunch

in the Horn and Horn family restaurant on Baltimore St., my family's former business. My favorite lunch, however, on the "Block" was a Polish hot dog with sauerkraut and mustard from a lunch stand. Little did I know that soon I'd be working as a guitarist on this "Block," part time.   One side effect of working downtown was that I got to be in court a lot, necessitating the purchase of many a new suit, to be indistinguishable from the attorneys.

There was no parking anywhere near my office, so I had to park about half a mile away down E. Fayette St. in a dangerous section. I felt I needed a gun, and fortunately my brother Bob had a .38 special long barrel he had confiscated in an arrest, and ran it through the NCIC system, and found it was a "cold piece," or it had no identification in the criminal system. So to be protected in my new suits I carried the pistol from car to office each day on the long walk. It was all quite illegal, but I didn't care, I didn't trust the downtown denizens, and was glad to have the protection.

My nightmare with Ms. Fielding was coming to an end when I got transferred to a general caseload position, under an effeminate gentleman by the name of Edward Cary Mc Donald. I didn't realize this was going from frying pan and into the fire, but I soon understood what the agents complained about, the numbers that were overwhelming. I had an initial caseload of 300! How was I to supervise 300, much less take care of the paperwork on this many probationers?! I spent an awful lot of time shuffling files in the office, when I was supposed to be out seeing clients at home and on the job. It was impossible to do any "intensive" supervision, since the worst offenders were not to be found, and searching for them used up all the time needed for the rest of the caseload. We needed a union, AFSCME, the American Federation of State County and Municipal Employees Union, a branch of Afof L CIO, the American Federation of Labor, the national union, was it. I joined and encouraged everyone I knew to join. We needed a serious meeting with management about these enormous caseloads. We got the meeting, and work was undertaken to reduce caseload size.

My top 40 band was in limbo for a little while, and we practiced only sporadically. In the meantime I had met Elvin "EJ" Jones, my black bass player friend, and he was in a trio called Ozone with James Rock, a guitarist. They worked the "Block" at a club called "Bootsys's". When James could not play I was asked in to jam in front of the strippers for several hours, until about one AM, or later. The pay was about $15 for the night, not much. It was in a way a good gig, in that almost everything was improvised, and stimulated by the naked bodies moving around in front of us. We played a lot of blues as you could well imagine.

From 1976 until 1978 I studied piano with James Houston and classical guitar with Michael Lawrence, Peabody graduate. They taught at Catonsville Community College, so I stuck with them once a week for four semesters. Michael Lawrence is now a successful film maker, and gave up performing. I learned a lot from him, but most importantly how to read music. In the background of everything I did with bands and in Parole and Probation, I took my lessons with Lawrence, and later with his student Andrew Thornton. I learned to play Bach, and Jazz Classic like Laurindo Almeida, which would serve me well about ten years later.

Vertebrae kept working as a foursome in '76, but soon we thought we needed a lead singer, and we found Richard Fitzgerald, a big guy with a bold voice. He had gigs, so we just rehearsed his songs with our songs and started working more frequently. He was a great addition to the band, and we agreed to go by the name the "New Stock Band." That year we played a New Year's Eve job down south of Baltimore County, and we were quite successful.

Anne and I started visiting my parents on Maryland's Eastern shore, at their farm. It was fun, and about this time I took up a new interest, in distance running. I was smoking a half pack of cigarettes a day, when I decided to do something about it seriously, long distance racing. My first race was through Baltimore City for eight miles, which I finished in about 58 minutes. I was on top of the world from this experience and committed to stop smoking, although it was to take more than one race for that to happen. And drinking. Well, that was just something I did after a good run.

Gary Slavinsky and I used to go out night clubbing during our Vertebrae days.

Drinking beer was a strong part of this club hopping, and disco was in full swing during this period. One night we ran into Cynthia and her girlfriend, who was the girlfriend of Henry Winkler, we learned. Her name escapes me now, but it was Cynthia I was interested in, anyway.

I followed her home, and about four AM we had sex, and then I drove the 45 minute drive back home. I had to be at work at 8:30AM, which I managed without a problem. Later that day I phoned Cynthia, and tried to arrange another meeting, which I did a few days later. She had a little boy also, but her man had left her. I stayed with her one more night, and then it was over, and I don't know why really. I wrote a song about her, called "Cynthia", in hard rock style.

The song never went anywhere. I never introduced it to the band. It was a kind of secret I kept until I forgot it, like the affair with it.

Throughout 1977 we gigged here and there, and made some money, but after Richard left us we auditioned female singers. We discovered Liz Harris, a remarkable vocalist of about our age, pushing 30. She rehearsed with us, and we were able to incorporate more jazz like pieces. I remember we played "Fever" by Peggy Lee and "Summer Time" by Gershwin. We played a few gigs with Liz, but for some reason she didn't stay with us. After Liz I started taking up the study of Electronics Engineering, and in February of '78 I was taking Electronics 101.

At that same time I was investigating transferring my job from Baltimore to the Eastern Shore.

XVI

SALISBURY 49

Back at Calvert St. the mood was not favorable for me to move, as my supervisor, Cary Mc Donald, was not too happy with my work performance, but he felt that to recommend me for the Eastern shore vacancy would be a way to get rid of me, so he did. I was extremely happy about getting out of the city, which was burning me out. Still, the numbers in the caseload were stacked against us, and my professional life was miserable. I interviewed in the Salisbury, Md. office, and I made a favorable impression. I never mentioned the difficulty with the Baltimore caseload (they didn't have those numbers problems here). Of course, it helped that my father was the Wicomico County Health Officer. I took the new job right away, and moved in my parents house, leaving Anne in Baltimore where she continued to care for Daniel and the house on Random Rd. The boys in the band were sorry to see me go, but I was profoundly tired of Baltimore, and didn't regret the break up. I commuted to Baltimore on the weekends while we sought a buyer for our house, so Anne could join me in Allen. Daniel's middle name came from the town. Anne started packing. I settled into the Salisbury Office of Parole and Probation.

I had to leave my nascent electronics study behind, and withdrew from solid state devises. Now my evenings would be spent at the "Flying Club" on the boulevard in Salisbury, drinking beer with Paul Hull and

Linda Powell, a pretty blonde coworker. Linda became my project, and one night I took her to the end of Cottman Rd. both of us drunk, and in my Impala.

The night was frozen, but we made out a little, but without real feeling, on the back seat, when she suddenly passed out, and I had to take her home. What's the point in being unfaithful if you can't manage to consume the affair?! That was it for me and Linda. Back at work we dealt with cases together, but no more on the lust front. I continued my interest in distance running, and took very long runs, sometimes for well over an hour on the beautiful back roads of Wicomico County. I thought I would try for the Boston marathon some day.

Anne and I sold our end house for $28,000, twice what we paid for it, so we had a big down payment for the next house. A coworker at the office took me to see a property in Sierra Manor in Parsonsburg, and I decided right there to buy. At $48,000 it was a three bedroom two story house with a fireplace and two thirds of an acre ground. It was brand new, never lived in! In January of '79 while Anne and I were still living with Mom and Dad we had a blizzard to beat all blizzards. It must have snowed four feet deep. We were snowed in on the farm with the quarter mile driveway completely impassable. We needed to contract a snow plow to get us out. What a snow fall!

We moved into Box 162 Sierra Drive in Spring '79, and we started looking for daycare for Danny so Anne could work. She found a job at Maryland State bank, and changed her career to their new accounts desk. She was happy about getting into something new. I hooked up with local Road Runners' club, and started taking communal runs on Sunday mornings at the Salisbury Park. I started my job at the Salisbury Office of Parole and Probation under a supervisor named Ron Savage, and didn't hit it off well with him. He was a bureaucrat's bureaucrat, who didn't like my reports, and regularly wanted me to rewrite them, for no other reason than he didn't like me personally. He spoke like a redneck, and the floor of his State car was littered with fertilizer, as he used it to transport manure out to his residence and farm on Spearin Rd. Using that car was a smelly business, and it didn't run right, either. He didn't maintain it properly. The contact requirements were a dead serious business in this office, and they superceded any client requirement. With this office checking off the boxes monthly was the main goal, to give the appearance of stability. So, the agents ran around the county collecting face to face contacts with no concern for the welfare of the clients themselves. As a result, many of them engaged in new criminal activity, and had to be reincarcerated. It was the "religion of paperwork", to quote some famous author or other. This is the way they played it when the management were agents, and they could not see any other way of supervising parolees and probationers. So, the supervisors strictly enforced the contacts standards.

It wasn't for nothing that I joined the union, and so when the representative asked me about stewardship I readily agreed to come on board as a shop steward. Most of the agents around me joined AFSCME, and at first it was no problem. When the issue of grievances came up it was a whole other matter. To be represented in a grievance procedure by a union representative was unthinkable to these people, the management, that is. One of my first actions here was to grieve an evaluation received from "farmer" Savage, and as redress I requested a new supervisor, which I got. I was transferred to Paul Hull, who was not terribly happy with the arrangement. He was a supercilious type, a Viet Nam veteran, who believed in most of the theories fed him by this management. He was an English major who took issue with the placement of commas, and parts of speech, and soon I had grievances with him. For a while, however, it all worked out, and we were drinking buddies.

The daycare we found for Danny, "Tiny Tots," was owned by a mother and son, who were most caring with their charges. Danny was now four years old, a dream child, and was soon to enter the kindergarden class at St. Francis de Sales Catholic school. Anne was well established in her first job at First Shore Federal on N. Division St., in downtown Salisbury.

She was two years later to be employed by Maryland State Bank on Salisbury Boulevard, where she became new accounts manager. In early 1980 Anne became pregnant with Aimee, who was born on November 30, 1980. Again I participated in natural child birth with Aimee.

I was running more and more, and losing weight to become ready for marathoning and 10 mile special runs, like the "Seaside 10" in Ocean City. I was covering the 10 K's and 10 milers with seven minute miles consistently. I was very happy. Then I discovered Ishinryu Karate with Tom Lewis at the Karate Barn on Old Ocean City Rd, near my home. I studied there until one of my parolees hit me in the rib cage, bruising me so hard I had trouble breathing for a time. I quit that Dojo after that, and found Shorinji Kempo, or a Japanese rendition of Shaolin Kempo, run by Dr. John Lee Stump, a chiropractor and a pilot. I had started seeing a chiropractor for my low back trouble which plagued me still, but running and exercise tended to help with the condition.

One day while I was visiting my parent's farm I looked over a yard sale, and found some books, one of which was from the sixties, called <u>You are All Sanpaku,</u> all about Macrobiotics. I devoured it, and commenced a serious study of the diet of macrobiotics, yin and yang philosophy. This philosophy, created by George Ozawa, dictated that yin and yang exist naturally in a proportion of five yin to one yang. Brown rice is therefore the perfect food since it represents the 5 to 1 ratio. I started eating only brown rice for about a month and lost 22 lbs.!

When my brother Bob saw me he thanked me "for coming down off the cross", I was so thin. Anyway, I took up the macrobiotics banner, and started to make dishes with whole grain foods, flax seed, millet, wheat berry, oats, barley and more. I was preaching to everyone I met about the healing and life giving powers of the macrobiotic regimen. I seemed to have damaged a nerve in my neck responsible for the nerves running down my right arm, and it left me kind of paralyzed in part of my right arm. Anyway, the macrobiotics seemed to have healed it, and after several months I was normal again. I continued running and working out in the Kempo dojo of the Drs. Stump and Stump. Eleanor was also a chiropractor and a black belt in Shorinji Kempo, as well. I worked my way up to brown belt, and brought Danny into it when he turned about nine. In 1980 I ran in the Annapolis 10 miler with my high school friend, Bob Bohnke, with whom I frequently trained, and who lived nearby, on Walston Switch Rd. I injured a calf in this race and didn't place very well. I ran it in 89 minutes. It was fun, and Aunt

Ruthette put us up for the night the day before the race. She lived with her husband, Charles, in Annapolis where he was a professor of English at the U.S. Naval Academy. She had three kids, Larry, Charlene and Louise.

When we came back East from California in '71 we brought Chloe, the mother, and babies, Pudge, Rudy and Sabrina with us. Pudge and Sabrina became my Mom's dogs, and Rudy went to John and Evie, but he ran away, unfortunately. Sabrina mated with a black Labrador, and she produced a litter out of which I got Bucky and Othello..Bucky died when he dragged home a fetid deer carcass. It apparently poisoned him. Othello stayed with me some years, and dear Chloe died one summer afternoon in 1984. Chloe was a wonderful golden Labrador, was very smart, and lived about fourteen years.

Paul Hull showed his true colors over time as my supervisor, and it was not long before my evaluations were less than satisfactory, despite all the outside approved training I received. As an example I went to train with Dr. William Glasser in his theory of Reality Therapy, a here and now based therapy for dealing with clients and children. Later, Dr. Dick Jontry gave a week seminar on Family Therapy after the Bandler - Satir model. He also taught and used Neurolinguistics, particularly with Viet Nam veterans. All these therapies were extremely informative, but returning to work armed with new methodologies made it almost impossible to stay at this office. It so outstripped their ancient ways of dealing with clients that new grievances arose. I was charged with disloyalty in the case of "Junebug" Jones, who told the Field Supervisor II that I was saying demeaning things about the management. I don't know how he came up with that, unless he was encouraged. This time the supervisor wanted a new supervisor in a different office for me. So I was transferred south to the Princess Anne, Md. office, working under Ron Mc Intyre, a Sergeant in the National Guard. I'm not sure that Ron wanted to be seen as a bureaucrat, but he was obsessive compulsive about order, and not much easier to get along with than Hull. I had guitar playing in common with him, though, and we got along initially quite well. The other agents in this office were a joy to be around and work with. My new caseload included the watermen around Deal Island. They were a hard drinking and fighting bunch, and my main responsibility with was seeing to it that they got to their local AA meetings, and keeping them out of bars. It was an interesting experience over all, and I continued in it for couple years until 1983.

One of my last experiences involved a client whose real name was "Prince Albert Baltimore". I was in his home one day discussing my martial art with him, and showed him some Tai Chi. I explained to him that solid objects could be removed with the powers of the mind through Tai Chi. I told him bricks could be moved out of place with the right force and cooperation from them. I showed him some exercises to compact the Chi, and told him that walls could be broken down with the right impact of a kick. He seemed sincerely interested in martial arts, and I suggested he could join me in my study of Kempo when he got off probation.

The next thing I know Prince Albert was reincarcerated for some minor offence. And then he escaped, by loosening the brick wall of the back of the jail. Wow, the power of suggestion is an awesome thing sometimes!

One mildly cold morning in February of '83 I came to work a little late, and discovered that my State vehicle had been taken before I got there. I had a whole day in the field planned, so I took off in my personal vehicle up to Salisbury when I experienced a panic episode complete with hyperventilation and chest pains, the likes of which I had never felt before. It was about nine AM, and I grabbed a six pack and downed two beers quickly to steady my nerves..It didn't work, and I went to the local hospital emergency. I was afraid I was having a heart attack.

The emergency physicians confirmed I did not have a heart attack, but wanted to admit me to be sure. I was to undergo a stress test, and I was visited by a Psychiatrist, the "gentle giant," Dr. Dick Kennan. He was indeed gentle and very large in stature, and he became my Psychiatrist for the next few years. I immediately I took sick leave, and stayed on sick leave until I resigned from the Agency. Apparently I suffered a delayed stress reaction, or Post Traumatic Stress disorder.

I passed my stress test without incident, so my heart was alright. It was all in my head! I had just held in a massive amount of stress over time dealing with the management, and I just broke down, rather than deal with their artificial standards any longer.

I hired an attorney and filed a workman's compensation case, in which I charged the management with harassment. I resigned my position effective June 1983, so I would have ten years of service. I wrote a very liberated letter of resignation, with the claim that I had been harassed, and could no longer function as a Parole and Probation Agent. At the same time I wrote a letter to the editor of the Salisbury Daily Times in which I claimed the management of Parole and Probation was "working out its own infantile hostilities on the community it served," by upholding the fallacious standards it wanted us all to subscribe to. Later my case went to trial, and it was established that indeed I had been harassed, awarding me a settlement of $15,000. For the time the award was substantial, and I planned to take off work for the next year.

My father was busy trying to make the county Health department more computer friendly, and doing what federal employees are famous for: "allocating funds". The local county council demanded he not reserve any of his budget for new computers and software to streamline his Health department. Over a period of months Dad bumped heads with various council members, and finally they retaliated by suggesting he was doing something illegal by virtue of his modernization program. After a time he found it impossible to compromise with them, and he resigned sometime around 1983. "Buchness resigns" read the headline of the Daily Times, and the lead article focused on the conflicts between county council and Health department.

During my time off from work I spent a lot of it up at the Delmarva Health Centre, taking acupuncture treatments from resident Oriental medicine doctor Hideyuki Ban, who had come from Japan, and was a black belt in Shorinji Kempo. He said all I needed was more "yang" in my diet. He treated several meridians with his needles, and he was right. I gradually got better with concentration on diet, by eating more meat, mainly fish and poultry.

I also spent more time practicing Kempo as much as possible to build up my strength and confidence. My techniques were improving, and I was advancing to second degree brown belt, the last rank before black.

I wanted to touch base with Erik Johnson in California, to see if he would help me financially, in order to sue the State of Maryland for harassment, seeking serious damages for loss of livelihood. Therefore, I judged a road trip to California was in order. Hide Ban was interested in seeing the West, and would come with me. It was around the first week of June we took off in my VW convertible, packed for camping out along the way. My wife was angry because I left both her and Daniel with the flu, but there was obviously nothing to be done but let the virus pass. I took the last vial of low dose stelazine I was prescribed with the intention of leaving it on top of one of the Rocky mountains, ceremoniously quitting it. I did that, and unfortunately immediately began to feel the need to drink beer as an alternative. Hide never joined me, and basically disapproved of my drinking. I was very much into the study and teaching of Hatha Yoga at that time, and a drinking regimen was not supposed to be part of a yoga teacher's life. I had gotten back to smoking pot, too. "All in moderation" my father always taught me.

When we got to Erik's we ate abalone, and drank fine wine. We went to a party on one of the nights, and I got seriously stoned on beer, wine and pot. Later, Erik produced the cocaine, and I went to the bathroom to snort a line or a half dozen lines. I met Erik's gardener, an attractive female who drank wine with me all the way back to house, and into the bedroom. Dr. Ban was staying in the same room with me, so it was a little uncomfortable for him, and he let me know of his disapproval, as always. Despite, we made love in an uninhibited way, and then the girl left for the night. I have never seen her since.

We hooked Erik up with the Sensei of Shorinji Kempo who lived in the general area, and Erik expressed a sincere desire to learn the martial art. Hide and I had demonstrated the fighting style in his back garden, and he was favorably impressed. Since that time Erik has studied to black belt, and sees Sensei Ota frequently. On the matter of financing my suit Erik was less than enthusiastic, and despite his abundant earnings as a dealer of cocaine he never helped me out. I went back home empty handed. Regrettably, I was never able to mount a case against the State of Maryland. The only consolation is a small retirement pension I receive each month.

Hide laid down the roots for his future on the trip, and today he has a successful chiropractic and Oriental medicine(acupuncture) practice in Northern California. On our trip we were able to visit my brother, Bob, who had moved to Denver with his second wife, Cathy. He took us up to Love Pass high in the Rockies where in June we ran in a snowfall. It was a refreshing experience, following all the partying I'd been doing. Bob had left his position as a Montgomery County Cop, and now was a sales rep for Johnson and Johnson in the Denver area.

"Observations, crossing the United States, June 1983"

"It used to be they cut the grass borders on both sides of the highways. Everywhere I go I notice that the center (median) strip is all that's cut, if that. Ten years ago you could picnic on the side of road- just plop down anywhere. Not now- the grass is no less than three feet high! (Everywhere!) Another distinctive feature are the fences-'used to be none- Everywhere across Reagan's U.S., about twenty five feet from the road, are fences! Fences around, and without a break, the Salt Lake and Nevada deserts- the mountains even! Can you imagine that somebody owns the Sierras? It is virtually impossible to camp anywhere today except at an $8 per night campsite(KOA or Good Neighbor Sam's). The distance needed to travel off the highway to find a chuirch yard or some such place not marked 'Private Property' or 'No Tresspasing' is too costly for the traveler.

Almost everywhere rivers have risen, or are overflowing. The Great Salt lake is now blue green, seen from high ground. Nevada is now a scene from another state. Water is everywhere, and so is green- very unlikely-very different from before. Three mile squares are covered by water!

Coming through Wyoming on June 14 in the evening it was about 35 degrees F!

Everywhere it is unseasonably cold. In Evanston, Wyo. on the way to California a rainstorm put a chill through my lungs I've never felt. It was as though the rain had been super cooled just above the immediate atmosphere, but defrosted just before it clobbered me, while in my poncho, filling my gas tank that evening.

Denver on the way home, 6/15/83, upon rising was sunny at about 40 degrees. It felt good, a little strange though for June."

XVII

YOGA FREE LANCE JOURNALIST MUSICIAN BAKER

I had written a scathing article about the Division of Parole and Probation to the Editor of the Salisbury Times, and as a result, got hired as a free lance journalist for the paper. My first assignment was to write about the various arts organizations on the Delmarva Peninsula. The series appeared in the Sunday paper for about five weeks straight, and I was thanked by many town fathers, who wrote to the paper in support of it. It was a good introduction to every artist and musician in the Delmarva region(the Eastern shore of Delaware, Maryland .and Virginia). After the series I reviewed the visiting Baltimore Symphony Orchestra, dance companies and theater productions as well as Civic Center Pop concerts. I interviewed visiting dignitaries to the University, like Carlos Fuentes, and was able to create my own features. For a time I had a weekly column called " On The Town". With shows I had to make the two AM deadline, and often fortified myself with a few beers. I was really enjoying my new part time career.

In San Francisco about 1967 I was introduced to Hatha Yoga by a returning Viet Nam Vet, George Kahn's older brother, Jeff Kahn. He taught me some basics about breathing and stretching, and later I got

Ernest Wood's <u>Yoga</u> in paperback. Jeff had been studying Paramahansa Yogananda's spiritual path, and I found a small booklet of aphorisms by him, which I meditated on. Later still, I found Sachidananda's book of Yoga, which I also studied.

I found more books of Yoga and devoured them. While I was still studying Shorinji Kempo my teacher was very impressed with my unusual flexibility, and hired me as the Yoga instructor for the Delmarva Health Centre. My students came from Kempo classes as well as from the general community. The classes were filled and quite successful. My earnings were substantial.

I was fortunate to have found Dr. Kennan, as mentioned earlier, and had the opportunity with him to engage in Psychoanalysis, as he had studied at the Institute of Psychoanalysis in the United States. I began writing out my dreams as I awoke in the mornings. One was of a lonely wooden cabin deep in the woods, which represented my isolation from the world around me. And, it represented, Dr. Kennan said, my survival. It was spooky. I kept Dr. Kennan as my psychotherapist for several years, until I left the Delmarva area in 1990.

Sadly Dr. Kennan contracted Parkinson's disease, and died in the late 1990's. It was a great loss to the psychiatric community.

I don't know who gifted me <u>The Tassajara Bread Book</u> by Edward Espe Brown, but for that I will be forever grateful. It was through Brown's book that I became interested in whole grain baking. I bought large steel bowls and baking tins, in order to produce four large loaves at a time, which I gave away to family and friends. One of my favorites to make was the rye-oatmeal bread, which I think is a healing bread. The Tibetan barley bread was also a favorite, and required quite a bit of work. Finding barley and rye flour today is quite a task. It used to be readily available in stores like the A&P and Food Lion, but not now. Today it must be special ordered from health food stores. I got familiar with so many breads that Dr. John Stump offered me a class teaching "Survival bread baking" at the Delmarva Health Centre.

Along with teaching yoga, baking breads and writing my newspaper articles I also found time to teach guitar at Salisbury Music, who provided me with a small studio. The pay was moderate, but it encouraged me to create some guitar repertoire for performance.

I started playing solo in restaurants around town, and later solo and with a band, in Ocean City, Md..

In 1984 I had one detour in my music career when I agreed to take a manager position for the new Jiffy Lube in Salisbury. Don Keyes was the general manager/owner who gave me the job. I hired the first crew and got off to a good start with an moderate income. The business took off in Salisbury, and is still standing today under new owners. It was a greasy messy job, despite the title, and after about six months I had a falling out with the owner over an innocent mistake and got fired. It wasn't really in the stars for me, I guess.

Anne was not too happy with me brokering several occupations, and wanted me to find a replacement for Parole and Probation, which I never did. I lived through many months of working dead end jobs for small pay, along with my personal interests. I took a job at a record store in the old mall called Camelot Music. I got lots of new music through 1985, but not a lot of income. Marketing LP's was still going strong through the end of the eighties. I lasted as a record store part time employee about a year. I became familiar with all the new artists of the eighties, the Pretenders, Billy Idol and Level 42 my favorite bands

Most of 1986 I split myself between Yoga, Journalism and music. I took up a part time engagement with the restoration of a Chris Craft cabin cruiser belonging to Dr. Stump. I spent a good deal of time stripping the finish off the boat, so that it cold be restored with a new finish. It was hard, monotonous work, and soon got old. At this time I was also preparing for the second degree brown belt test in Kempo. I worked with Randy Parsons, a Correctional Officer at the Westover prison. He and I became close friends, bonding as we did with the martial art, and me teaching him Yoga. I branched out with my Yoga program by offering a course to multiple sclerosis victims at the Holly Center in Salisbury, and at a health and fitness center on Milford st. in Salisbury. At the fitness center I met my friend, Stefan Cameron, a carpenter, and a devotee to Sri Chinmoy, the runners'' guru. I first met Stefan with his wife Nina at the Yoga class I was to teach, but that never materialized for lack of students. Stefan asked me what I did for a living, and I explained how I tried to earn enough from writing, Yoga teaching and playing music sometimes. He asked me if I wanted to help him in his construction business, since his helper had quit on him. I decided learning carpentry would be a worthwhile occupation, and joined him as a helper. Although this was another detour from my music career Stefan paid me fairly, and the hours were good. We normally got underway around 7:30AM and quit by 4PM. I discovered what a joy this fellow Yoga enthusiast was to work with. We often listened to tapes we both brought to the job site. He brought music from disciples of Guru Sri Chinmoy, and I found them stimulating, especially the womens' singing group called Akasha. We traveled up to Washington, D.C. one weekend to see them and meet with them. They were Swedish, and spoke perfect English. They sang like angels, and I had to find out more about this guru Chinmoy, who had attracted such a following. I found out other disciples included the pop singer Carly Simon, and several Olympians.

By 1987 Anne was showing signs of being fed up with me and my jobs that didn't provide a good living for the family, and we argued. In July she planned a visit to her family in Biloxi, Mississippi. She said she would be gone for three weeks, but never returned back home. I would call down there and I was told she was in therapy with someone, and didn't plan to come back. She was severely depressed, and wanted a divorce. The long lonesome necessary twelve months separation had begun. From then on I was to live without my two kids, Daniel and Aimee. In the Fall I drove, with my Dad, down to Mississippi to visit the children.

We drove over to New Orleans for a day trip with the kids and had a good time, eating and sightseeing. Anne did not seem to want to reconcile, and Dad and I drove quietly back to Maryland. I felt defeated.

How I paid my mortgage for the next two years is a mystery to me now. My savings were almost used up, music jobs were few and far between, journalism paid some bills, and Yoga classes were fewer and fewer. I applied for every professional job I came across, but got no offers. I was still seeing Dr. Kennan, and he wondered why I didn't pursue music full time. I took that suggestion seriously, and began practicing and auditioning personnel for a rock trio, along with solo guitar and vocal gigs. I started getting a few solo gigs.

1988 started new fortunes for me, as I found a job writing for Ocean City Magazine, the magazine of real estate, which focused on entertainment and tourism. My first assignment was about the traditional entertainers who visited the shore in the summer season.

I got to interview the Righteous Brothers, the Diamonds, Kenny Rodgers, Chubby Checker, and several more. The articles really helped me pay my bills, at about $500 per article. At that time it was a lot of money.

I found a guitar partner from Pittsburg, Pa., Ray Moreton, who recently moved to the beach. He had some good experience playing with a top 40 group in Pittsburg that was successful enough to record a single, a song Ray wrote. I didn't like the song much, but I did like Ray's guitar playing, and we soon formed a trio with an eighteen year old drummer who could play everything. I got us full time work at Salvatores at 10th and Boardwalk, and we were booked for the summer. No more money problems, for a while at least. Plus we played out onto the Boardwalk. It was a blast, in which I got to play bass while Ray played guitar, and vice versa.

We played Bo Diddly, Buddy Holly, Elvis, the Beatles and the Doors, and much more, even Dire Straits and Rod Stewart. The nicest part of this summer was Anne sending my kids by plane up to Maryland for vacation. I got to stay with them for a week, and I bought Danny a bass guitar and small practice amp to take back home. I even kept them up late one night at the restaurant to hear me play. I felt ecstatic. I missed them all so much. Then I drove them to the airport and saw them off, Danny 13 and Aimee 6 at the time.

By Labor Day the First Wave Trio broke up, and I started waiting tables for Salvatore, where I made more money in tips than from my music job! I worked there for a month or so, then started looking for new sidemen for the next incarnation of the First Wave Trio. That's when I met Roger Henry, the classical guitarist, bassist and singer. As a Duo we played Christmas dinner parties and small clubs, and then we found our Drummer, Gary Ostrowski, and booked into the old Johnny's and Sammy's restaurant and night club. The trio did not last but we did book some studio time at Seagull studio of WSCL Radio, and recorded the "Guitar Boogie Shuffle" by Clarence Smith and "Love's Made a Fool of You" by Buddy Holly. Both songs were owned by Paul McCartney's publishing company, and I called his office to get permission to record them. They were both good recordings, and I still have a digital analog cassette tape of them. I encouraged local radio to play them, but did not get any positive response from DJ's.

My next move was to apply for a substitute teacher position around Salisbury, which I got, and started substituting on a regular basis. Being with the kids made me feel good, as I was reminded of my own. I stayed with it through the school year, and at the end of the year picked up a bass player and drummer who were graduating seniors. We played a few nights in Ocean City, and for a graduation party around town. They were amazingly clever for eighteen.

The band broke up when they went off to college, and I went back to substitute teaching. Then I got the itch to travel, because I was depressed missing my kids. I sold the house, packed up my essentials for gigging in a VW bus, and took off for Sebring, Florida, where

Anne had moved with her new boyfriend. It was a murderously cold that winter, and I was glad to go to a warmer place, but I got fooled. There was an unusual ice storm in Sebring. I found a caretaker position and an apartment to go with it. I was to do basic maintenance, and I found two music jobs, one in the best restaurant in town, and a teaching/faculty position at South Florida

Community College, teaching classical guitar part time. I started playing and singing solo in the restaurant and teaching for about a month, and was doing well, when Anne's lawyer got a warrant for my arrest for "telephone abuse." This was following a conversation I had with this Mr. Kelley, in which expletives were used by me, as I was so angry at the custody arrangement they had come up with. He had me picked up and locked up by cops with ouzis from my apartment. The bail was set at about one hundred dollars, and I called my brother to help me out as I was short on cash. The next day after bail was posted I was so upset I packed up my van and my dog Othello, and started back to Salisbury, humiliated terribly.

Driving North to Orlando I felt so tense and anxious I decided to do the only thing I knew: stop in at a hospital. I asked to see a psychotherapist, and saw instead some intake coordinator. I waited a long time when two sheriff's deputies rushed in and grabbed me, put me in a van, and I was taken to a psychiatric lock up somewhere in Orlando. I had no idea what to say when I got there, and I tried to explain how I applied to talk with a counselor, that I didn't belong in this lock up. Nobody listened to me it seemed, and they tried to force pills on me they called "meds." I tried to tell the attendant I didn't need any "meds", and they nearly jumped on me to force me. I stayed calm, and they finally let me go to a free area in the middle of the large room.

I mingled, or rather, stood around observing the large group. Nobody seemed normal, and it hit me hard that I was in a loony bin. An attendant showed me to a bed, and my neighbor there made strange diving motions trying to get my attention, and saying something to the effect that he was flying. I lied down and he left the room, and it was late, about 9:30PM. The next day I was told that I would have a chance to see the doctor, a psychiatrist. About eleven o'clock that morning I finally talked with the doctor, and tried to explain to him this was a mistake. I showed him my business card, my guitar card, that I had in my pocket. I told him I played in restaurants, and that I planned to see if there were a spot for me to play in Orlando. I told him about my therapist, Dr. Kennan, and he gave him a call and told Kennan my story. I was immediately scheduled for release, and I got to leave. I found a bus stop and directions back across town to the hospital, where I asked where my van was. It was impounded, and I was able to get it out without charge. But, my dog was impounded at the "pound", which I had to find and went and got him out. It was 4PM by this time, and I applied to a French restaurant for the night, but no luck, although it was a very nice place, and I would have liked to play some of my classical repertoire there. So, I decided to get driving through the night back to Maryland. I slept that night in a rural Georgia community where

I pulled on a vacant lot, and fell fast asleep in my little bed, actually a futon mattress.

I woke up at first light and continued on my way through the Carolinas until late afternoon when I reached the southern portion of Virginia. Virginia is a big state, and it was late in the evening when I reached Washington, D.C.. My destination was my sister, Evelyn's home on Bel Bluff rd. in Gaithersburg, Md.. I arrived after midnight, and woke my brother in law, Hank, with all my problems. I couldn't believe the experience of the last 72 hours, and so I determined to write it out while it was fresh in memory. Somewhere there is a self pitying written long hand account of my incarceration and confinement, in one of my notebooks. What a whirlwind it was! My sister gave me $120 in cash and sent me on my way back to the shore, where I had no friends or lodging. I went to my parents place on Fairway Drive in Ocean Pines.

My friend Stefan had moved to Ithaca, N.Y., where he found a nice home, and work contracts.

I searched the want ads for lodging, and came across a room with an elderly gentleman about eighty five years old. I took the room, but had no idea what an adventure rooming with this old codger would hold. We both smoked pipes together, and at first things were alright. Little by little, however, this man came to possess me. He wanted to control my comings and goings, and wanted me to join him in his social activities with the senior center! With him I had absolutely no privacy, and had to get away. The only problem was the unusually cold March, and I couldn't sleep in my van. I finally found a room with Henrietta Moore and her psychiatric son who had just lost his father with whom he was very close. It was in Salisbury on Johnson Lake, a nice setting, and a good place to practice classical guitar and write. My newspaper job had pretty much dried up with my absence from Salisbury these few months. Substitute teaching was not available at the time, as I had no telephone.(This was in the days before cell phones). I took a job at Survival Products, a family business run by a nice young couple. I was hired to recondition and repair kerosene heaters, and do minor carpentry to install wood stoves. I never got that far, when I broke down with a depression from missing my two kids, and had to resign with the story that I was leaving town for Florida, which was half true. I called up Stefan Cameron about staying with him for a time, and after a bad confrontation with Mrs. Moore's son at the house, we decided that it would be to our mutual benefit for me to find other lodging. First, however, I recorded my classical and jazz moods pieces with my cousin, Michael John, who had a digital analog cassette deck, and we worked together for several days compiling what would be the best demo tape I have ever recorded. He was a great help to me, as I needed a decent demo to show to restaurants and bars along my road. I am very grateful to him.

I said goodbye to my Mom and Dad, and took off for upstate New York near the beginning of June, 1990. I had packed my van with all my earthly belongings except for that which I put in storage with my brother Bob in Wilmington, De.. I gave him all my clothing, my stereo and records collection, and some furniture I wanted to keep. I didn't know when I'd be back for any of it, and it turned out he kept it all for five years. I think I borrowed some money from him to get on the road. I took off with my dog Othello, and arrived on the mountainside in Ithaca around the second of June. I had looked for his place through the night, and discovered there had been a murder recently in one development I searched. I pulled over on the side of the mountain road, tucked my .38 caliber revolver under my seat, and fell asleep in the driver's seat.

Early next morning I was abruptly awoken by the sound of some rapping on my window. I immediately reached for the Smith & Wesson, holding it in his face. Then I awoke really and saw Stefan's face before me, thank God. He noticed my van on the mountainside and stopped.

Again, this was in the days just before the cell phone and gps revolution, so finding one another was awkward. I followed Stefan to a lovely place set on a hillside with a pond, his new home. He had made it beautiful with new carpeting and baths.

I slept on his living room floor on my bed from the van. I stayed with the Camerons for about a week, until I found part time work playing at a local restaurant, the chef of which was from South America. His name was Jaramillo. I played Friday and Saturday nights for $35, enough to pay the rent on my room at the Dryden hotel, slightly outside Ithaca, in Dryden. There was icy rain up here on the fifth of June, so I was glad to find a warm place to stay. I decided to drive up to Montreal to see about music work up in that fabled city. I got to the border crossing and they asked me if I had any guns? I automatically answered no, not wanting to give up my personal protection while on the road. They decided to ransack my van, and they discovered my .38 caliber revolver and my .25 caliber automatic. They confiscated my guns and told me I owed them a $200 fine. They also ran a criminal records check on me, and fortunately missed the outstanding warrant I had on me for my failure to appear in the telephone abuse case in Florida. All I had left was two hundred dollars, so I was busted. Fortunately, I still had credit cards for gas and an American Express card. I was not welcome in Canada, so I turned around my junked contents-(they really made a mess!)- and went back to Stefan's with my sad story. He told me I "told you so", being the anti gun person he was. I did miss my .38 smith & Wesson especially.

It was time to travel south, back to Florida, and to my kids. My plan was to get established as a musician, hire a lawyer to straighten out my case, and see my kids. Anne had divorced me in absentia the previous winter, so I had no chance to represent myself, but the only issue was visitation rights, which she never denied, anyway. The big problem was child support that was seriously in arrears. So work was paramount. I went to Coconut Grove, where I found a chance to play in the Trattoria in the Grove for tips. I met "Pancho," Francisco Dudas, working there as a waiter. He was actually a finished doctor from Peru, who needed a residency at a hospital. I found construction work on the new multi theater that was being built. Pancho helped me a little with moving sheets of steel to the second floor. I got him paid as casual labor to overcome the immigration issue. I went to work during the day as a carpenter building the floors of the movie theaters. It lasted about three weeks before I got mysteriously fired after working with a pair of black guys who were less than competent as carpenters. For some reason the supervisor was told that I was incompetent. Oh well, so much for politics!

I pulled enough money together to make a deposit on an apartment on Second st. in South Beach. Miami. I rented from a friendly Cuban family, and even got Pancho into the apartment next door to me. The rents were cheap then in south Beach, unlike today. There was a food hand out in the neighborhood where Pancho and I got canned goods we could eat by heating up in our little kitchens. We certainly missed the free meals we got at the Trattoria in the Grove. Having paid the rent I was flat broke, and my dog and I were literally starving until I got my first playing job at the Carlisle one night a week on Ocean Drive. The deal I made at the Carlisle was $20 per night plus dinner for me and a lady friend, should one appear. It helped pay for my gas, so I could look for more jobs. I latched onto a job carrying temporary workers to their job sites very early in the morning, so I was getting up at four AM, after working to eleven PM some nights. I found a second music job at another hotel that Scandinavian Airlines System (SAS) used for their "Star Tours," package deals for Danes, Swedes and Norwegians. I played Friday night parties for their guests, who were I might add, extremely lively. It was almost too much sometimes, when they got their swords out and danced on the tables in mock battles. Extremely inebriated was an understatement to make of them! In my pop repertoire I had a good number of lively tunes to play. They loved me.

I had three nights to fill in and I got to seeking work in the want ads of the Miami Herald. I came across an interviewer position for Florida Public Information and Research Group, PIRG, run by Ralph Nader. The pay was good and the hours flexible. I joined them as soon as I could. We would canvass neighborhoods fund raising, to raise public awareness of the danger the big oil companies were making along the Florida coastline, and its ecosystems. We canvassed all over Miami up through Ft. Lauderdale. I was doing great at the job when we entered a wealthy neighborhood that required background checks on any of us who came into it.

That was the end of Florida PIRG for me due to that outstanding warrant for my arrest from Highlands County Court in Sebring. I was able to find another night at the Betsy Ross Hotel on Ocean Drive, the headquarters for models and celebrities. I played there several nights for good wages, until a duo came in and usurped my position. I should have gotten a contract, but didn't.

One night I went over to the ice cream parlor in South Beach, when I met a black woman on a bicycle who was stunning. We met and talked a while, and I told her about my bike, an Eddie Merx. We agreed to ride together, and I invited her back to my place, where we made out, and she performed fellatio on me. I was in heaven. Later we rode our bikes together, and I eventually visited her home and child. She was a bank examiner, and a graduate of Dartmouth, I think it was. Adriene was her name, and we made furious love at her place one night. She visited me one afternoon that I had to play, and we did it again. That night I played like an angel. I had to borrow $75 from Adrienne to pay my rent. I liked Adrienne, but she told me her parents would never approve of us, the racial barrier was the thing.

XVIII

CHARLOTTE, COPENHAGEN, 15 MINUTES OF FAME

It was late August,1990, and I was about to meet the love of my life, the woman I would spend the rest of my life with, Charlotte Lerche. One night I went out shopping at the local Pantry Pride with my dog, Othello, 'Thello for short. Naturally, he stayed in the van when I went inside. I spotted her when I picked up my half gallon of ice cream. She was wearing a heavy cotton shiff that accentuated her fine back side. A local nut I'd seen around followed me into the store, and let me know in his way, that she was fine. I didn't think more about her, but when I got to the checkout there she was ahead of me in line. I looked at her, and asked her if she were Irish? She said "No, I'm Danish". I noticed that in her hand she held a packet of chewing gum and a can of beer. I thought "what a strange combination". She paid for her beer and gum, and waited for me to get through the checkout. I told her I was a guitarist, and then the conversation got rolling. She asked me if I wanted to go for a walk on the beach with her. Of course I did!

I asked her to ride with me in the van so I could drop my groceries at home. That was when I noticed Othello had raided my fresh new pizza

I had bought. He had eaten it all! And he did not approve of a woman being in the car with us. He growled at her, he was intensely jealous.

Intuitively he knew that she was a possible threat to him.

After dropping off the groceries we walked the beach and she told me of her desire to become an architect, and that she was in school full time for it. I told her I was something of a carpenter, and how I enjoyed construction, at least the end product of it. She was staying at the Imperial Hotel on Ocean Dr. and Fifth st. I told her about my music job at the Carlisle, and invited her to dine there with me. It got late, but time seem to pass unnoticed with Charlotte. At the end of our evening she asked me if I would like a little kiss, and then she gave me one elongated kiss. I think that was when I fell in love with Charlotte, that first night, I fell hard. I was still seeing Adrienne though, and that was problematic. I had a date with Adrienne the next afternoon, and then dinner with Charlotte. Talk about an embarrassment of riches! Two beautiful women, and I had to choose. I met with Adrienne that afternoon, we talked and maybe we made love. I expected to see Charlotte at the restaurant a little later, and when Adrienne walked out to leave, here comes Charlotte, walking up the drive! Now, I was just *plain* embarrassed!

We went out to dinner, had a great meal, then I played while Charlotte sat and listened. Before that, however, during dinner I told her that I swam daily at the beach at second street. The waiter, my good friend, told me they had spotted a great white shark about 8 ft. long at least around there. Oh, well. After dinner she and I went back to my place for the night. She had a terrible sunburn, and our first sexual contact must have been painful for her. Somehow we managed to both sleep on my little single bed comfortably. In the morning she was still red as a beet. We went over to the cool air conditioning of her hotel room. (My apartment had no air conditioning) Charlotte showered and got naked in the bed, which started something, and we stayed indoors for a good while that day. She had trips planned with her tour group in a motor coach. One of these was into the Florida Everglades. I wish I could have gone. I spent every day with Charlotte, excepting the planned trips with her tour group. Together we went to "Sea World" park one day, and later, over to the Miami marina and shopping mall, where Charlotte picked up necklaces for her friends. But, first we took a road trip to Key West in the van.

We planned a whole day on the road, and packed lunches. I packed extra water for drinking. It was a long trip, and the weather was nice. We got on the road by about 11:30AM.. We drove for a while and had lunch We surveyed the beautiful Keys as we drove past.

When we arrived we visited land's end where the sign reads"90 miles to Cuba." Then we went back to the bar Hemingway drank in, was it called Sloppy Joe's? By the time we found Hemingway's house it was just five o'clock and closed. Charlotte was severely disappointed, and blamed it on the early morning sandwich making that I had insisted on. We walked around the outside of the house and looked in the windows. It was just an old house to me....

We arrived late back in Miami Beach, having talked all the way back home about everything possible. I think I might have slept with Charlotte at the hotel that night. It was either the next day, or the day after that she had to leave, and it caused me to start smoking cigarettes again. Like I said, time seemed to stand still when I was with Charlotte, and having her taken from me caused me to regress with old abandoned habits like smoking. We vowed to see each other again and to write letters. Waving her goodbye from her motor coach following our last kiss was traumatic for me, and I had no idea how close we had become in a few short days together. A week later Charlotte called me on the phone of my land lord, and it was very good to hear her voice. I had stopped seeing Adrienne obviously, but still owed her $75, which I planned to pay through my land lord. I worked for another month until October, jogging some days for forty five minutes in the Miami heat. Pancho found a position working for a high school football team, as team doctor. I guess it was enough for his visa and green card. After I left Miami I lost touch with him I am sad to say, he was a special guy.

The music work seemed to dry up, though I did try to branch out with gigs outside the Beach area, without much success. I continued my relationship with SAS Star Tour parties.

Charlotte wrote to me as she promised to do, and I got great joy from her letters. She asked me to come to Denmark, and I thought about very briefly before I came to the conclusion that I could not live without her. My friend Stefan Cameron had predicted that I would meet a dark haired girl and fall hard. What an intuition that man had! I asked Charlotte for enough money(about $600) to finance my last months rent, pay Adrienne back and fly to Copenhagen. Then I went to the music store and sold all my gear, with a net gain (with the sale of my VW bus) of about $1700. Despite my taking good and long runs I was smoking a lot near the end of my stay in Miami.

I had to take Othello to the humane society, and had a very sad experience saying goodbye, but knew it was the right thing to do. Somehow I knew that he would understand, although my last caress of him was bittersweet, indeed. He had been with me for more than ten years. I also said goodbye to Pancho, and wished him success in his new country. My brother, Bob, sent me a *bon voyage* gift of $150, so I bought a Sony double cassette boom box to take with me, a wise investment. I went to a shipping company and packed my belongings in a crate to go by boat.

I set aside a plane ticket and was able to fly for $140 because I received an employee discount. My departure date, I think, was October 10th. In any case, it was a hot day that late afternoon, about 3:30PM when we boarded the motor coach that would take us to the airport. After a couple hours of flying we landed in Bangor, Maine, where we experienced cold weather, and a duty free shop. I think I purchased a pack of cigarettes. From there at about eleven o'clock we boarded the SAS jetliner where all the overhead language was in Danish or Swedish. I tried hard to understand any of it, without success. I tried to get to sleep, but we were headed into the sun, so I didn't get much. I remember the orange roof tops of Copenhagen, and my excitement grew. When we landed I was greeted by a smiling Charlotte, who had one segment of her hair braided back, and she looked particularly attractive. The cop who interviewed me told me "we don't need any more musicians in Copenhagen". He finally passed me through with my tourist visa, admittedly an icy welcome.

My next move was in Charlotte's "best" male "friend's" (if that's possible) Land Rover, getting packed in with the smallest amount of space. I met Alan Pedersen, who became also one of my best friends in Denmark. The ride home was mercilessly uncomfortable, and I was sure glad to get out of that small car. I had all my playing equipment with me, and that car was packed to the brim. We arrived at the apartment and mounted the three stairwells to the "anden etage", or second floor, where Charlotte rented a small but comfortable three room flat, with cold water only. This was actually the third floor, since the ground floor is not considered, and the third floor is called the second. There was a public bath fifty paces from the apartment, for which we would buy a booklet of tickets, and go in when we wanted a shower or a sauna bath. It was actually quite nice, and rarely overcrowded.

When I arrived the temperature read 16 degrees Celsius, about sixty something Fahrenheit, and it was pleasant. Early on I took a long distance run through the city to get acquainted with the streets, and of course, I got lost, and had to ask someone how to get back to Udebygade. "Gade" is a street. I got back just before dark, and the temperature dropped considerably. I had worn only a nylon shorts, and sleeveless nylon racing shirt. It was not enough. I was slowly to learn about the cold in Denmark. The first thing you needed to know was to wear a neck scarf at all times. Charlotte got me a pair of those from the Arab shops. She also had me buy new corduroy trousers and a light jacket.

We adapted to the makeshift bed Charlotte slept on- it was a mattress suspended over wooden beer boxes on the floor. It was rather lumpy, and I set about to buy us a real bed . I was able to find us a one piece mattress with built in box spring, a vast improvement. After having a good place to rest I set about to looking for performing work in restaurants. My first job was at the "Mexicali," a Mexican restaurant owned by a half American Dane named Kim Jacobsen. He spoke perfect English, and learned to cook in Southern California when he was a teenager. He was an excellent cook, and did justice to the Mexican menu. I got a job playing on Wednesday evening, and I tried to play Spanish classical, mostly student pieces. Kim stocked the place with good wines, and he did a good business. It was a fun place to play. It sat on a prominent corner on the Aboulevard, the big boulevard into the downtown city hall.

I continued to look for more work, and came upon another restaurant on Aboulevard, but closer to the city hall. It was a Danish restaurant called the "Salt and Pepper,"

Salt og Peber in Danish. It was in the basement, but was very nice. You stepped down from the street to come inside. I got hired by the manager, whose first name was Regner, the Danish equivalent of Rene. I was to play Thursday through Saturday nights, so I was getting really busy.

I needed to replace my $400 Senheiser microphone that was stolen by an employee of the Carlisle in Miami. I never could prove it, but the manager was sure it was him. It was a big mistake to leave expensive mikes on the premises when I was off. I should have known better.

I got the same mike, but it cost me a pretty penny, or should I say *crown*? I played everything I knew at Salt and Pepper, and there was a lot of drinking and partying after work. Back in Salisbury I had found AA, and worked the first four steps, but I'm afraid I fell off the wagon with the Salt and Pepper crowd, which started a slow downhill spiral.

By November 1990 things were moving very fast with Charlotte and my relationship. I think we both felt love for each other, and wanted to stay together. Anyway, my three month tourist visa was about to end. My family was appalled at the idea of a wedding after only three month's acquaintanceship. I didn't care, I wanted to stay here and be married We decided to marry December 16, and went to take blood tests for the marriage certificate. I went to my embassy to get proof of my divorce from Anne, and all was in readiness for the wedding. Our plan was to marry in the Trinitatis Church, built in 1642 by King Christian IV. It was built in a large tower that had a spiral ramp up to the top that the king would ride his horses up, very exciting! Being married assured me of permanent residence and a work permit. I had met Carmen, Charlotte's hard loving and hard drinking mother and her boyfriend, Kurt. We got together on regular evenings, and the Danish "welcome drink" was not lost on me. Carmen was a great cook.

The wedding was planned for the two of us, but we found out that legally we needed two witnesses. Kurt and Carmen became our two witnesses, and after that the group grew to twenty people! So we had a large wedding party, and Charlotte cooking and baking the wedding cake for us all. It was a carrot cake in a very large rectangle, a lot of work, to be sure. I had one blue suit that I brought, and the only pair of shoes I had other than running shoes. When I knelt in the church, the hole with the duct tape showed up on camera. It may have been embarrassing, but it reminded me of all the miles I'd walked with my guitar seeking work. That was a lot of pavement!

Charlotte was at school from 9AM to 9PM every week day, studying architecture in a building called Charlottenborg, one of the Queen's former castles, converted to a university.

Sometimes I would visit her once I had a bike to ride. We went up to the north coast of Sjelland to visit the Louisiana art museum. You could look at the North Sea and see the coast of Sweden.

I told Charlotte I was going to swim that crossing. She thought I was crazy, but it was one of my desires as a disciple of Sri Chinmoy, a means of showing my aspiration. I never did it, though.

Well, I was working four nights a week now, and actually getting press. The Salt and Pepper was an excellent Danish restaurant with a great menu, and it became very popular. Manager, Regner, definitely had a problem with drink, and always delayed my wages. I would chase him around to collect each week. The wine sellers had the same problem. The chef was the only one who got paid on time. He never cheated me, fortunately, and always considered me his good friend, but it sure was hard getting money out of him. He finally ran the business down, and before long had the authorities after him for tax and VAT evasion. I joined the Danish Musicians Union, which really protected its members.

Charlotte and I get married on December 16, 1990, and I applied for permanent residency, which I got for the next ten years. Before Christmas I changed jobs and started playing in a place called the Lumskebugten, or the "sneaky bay" restaurant. It was run by a Sri Lankan manager named Upali. He was a character, but always treated me good. I worked any night that people came in, and I'd get called in by telephone. I contracted another gig on Saturdays at a posh restaurant called Kommandanten, or the Commander. There I played unamplified, again in a basement step down. Dinner was part of my contract, and the meals were very excellent, from the best chefs in town. I was treated like royalty here, and the pay was good For example, I was transported to and from home by taxi compliments of the management.

This was located on Gronnegade in NyHavn, or new harbor, the nicest part of town, near the Danish Royal Theater. I was beginning to get starstruck.

I remember the Kommandanten being at the end of the "stroget", or walking street, so famous for its entertainers, I myself among them from time to time. This was where all talented people came to seek an audience, and this included buskers, circus performers, mimes, dramatic actors speaking their roles, comedians, puppet shows, and small music combos like skiffle bands. It was a magical place, like no place else in the world. If you went down to "stroget" in a depressed mood very shortly you'd alter it with the abundance of stimulation. It was where you'd meet people from every country night time and daytime. And, it was over a mile long! It was a fabulous tourist attraction, absolutely vibrant. It was where the Danish King Christian IX rode through on horseback during the Nazi occupation to cheer the populace. It was not unusual to see royalty on the streets in Copenhagen today even, and once Charlotte and I observed Prince Henrik walking his dogs down the street without escort, just like a normal citizen.

During this period I attended classes in "Danish for Foreigners" at nine o'clock in the mornings, Monday through Friday. I became friendly with the instructor, Gerard Schroeder, and sometimes went to dinner at his place. He was a good teacher and was very sympatico. He made me a wedding gift of a contemporary Danish ceramics painter, a small dish with three obelisks painted on the surface, something I have kept to this day.

The Christmas party came to Lumskebugten, and all the staff got together one night before the holiday. They asked me to play, and I brought my small amp and an electric guitar. Upali and his group took over the mike with a lot of foolishness. Everybody was drinking heavily, me included, and when the cook, Johnny, insulted me by telling me that my music stank, I took a swing at him. That was my last night at Lumskebugten, as Johnny informed the management that I lost my temper under drink. In Denmark that's the one thing that's not tolerated. Everybody drinks, but if you become angry, they draw the line.

I saw it sitting full on the table, and decided to drink the glass of red wine. It had strange bouquet about it, but I drank it down. I packed up my gear into my wagon and bike, and headed home. I felt pretty wasted from the drink, but I didn't know the half of it. When I hit the cool air I wanted to pass out, and in fact I tried to drive my bike and wagon, and just fell over. Two policemen picked me up off the pavement, got me to my feet so I would roll the bike and load down the street. A little wobbly, I stayed erect and got along my way to Udebygade.. Someone had spiked the wine and left it on the table! My guess was Qualude, but whatever it was, it was strong! I talked to my self all the way home as though I had a partner to my conversation. It was the strangest drunk I ever experienced, and I should have known better. I got my equipment up the three flights of stairs, said good night to Charlotte, and passed out.

I found a new job at La Capo Rojas, across the street from the Danish National Symphony Orchestra's Hall on Thursday nights. It was a nice Spanish restaurant, and at the end of the night I got to eat with the staff. One night in the middle of a song the Danish Police raided the place for illegal workers, and went directly to the kitchen. I don't know if they caught anybody without proper papers, but it certainly intimidated me. For some reason they never asked me for mine! It was here one night that I met Denmark's premier magician, "Kell."

He liked my playing, and invited me to play his birthday party in Kalenborg, about 50 kilometers distant from Copenhagen. So, one Saturday Charlotte and I trained over to Kalenborg, to a place called the Gilleleje restaurant. It was a nice feast, and Kell had pyrotechnics, flames shot from his fingertips! I drank one too many beers, and by the time I made it back to my gig at Kommandenten, Lars sent me home because he smelled it on me. So I got the night off, embarrassing.

By the end of March, 1991 I had the chance to audition for a full time gig at the SAS Royal, Copenhagen's elite hotel. I found out the pianist was vacating the Royal for the SAS hotel in Bergen, Norway. I immediately applied, and got an audition before the general manager. I dressed in coat and tie, and played a little classical and a little jazz, "Nature Boy." He liked me, and I got a contract for the month of April. The pay was about $5000 for the month, a royal sum indeed for '91. I immediately bought a VW Golf, and started restoring it. It turned out to be not such a good buy, for it was rusted in the under body. It cost me about $1600, but I couldn't get it to certify at the end of the year due to the rust. I had a lot to learn about the Danish wet weather effects on vehicles, and it wouldn't pass safety inspection. I drove it until early '92, and gave it away for about two hundred dollars at the last. Although I actually did not invest additional money in the car, I joined a so-called "Fritids Club", or free time club, for a small joiner's fee and replaced the rack and pinion steering by myself. It was possible at this government sponsored operation to do ceramic art, leather crafting, even recording in a studio for music, along with auto workshop and metal workshop. My installation of the rack and pinion nearly outshined the portable shower and hot water heater I installed at the apartment, by drilling through a wall, and running the hose through it. It worked, however, and we had hot water and hot showers in our bedroom. I probably violated all the Danish building codes by what I did, but we never told anybody in authority about it. When we left the apartment a few years later we explained to the new tenant what to look out for, and how to use it properly. I never heard anything bad about it, so I guess it worked out for him.

Now that I was established at the Hotel Royal I got my "fifteen minutes of fame" promised me by Andy Warhol. I had my name in lights after twenty years of practicing. It felt good. My next project was a Sunday paper route, after playing Saturday night I went out and delivered Sunday papers to Norrebro, or "North bridge", the community we lived near. This lasted until daylight Sunday morning. Climbing up six floors sometimes was really tiring, but good cardio exercise, to be sure. Fortunately, I had Sundays and Mondays off to recuperate and rest. As the weather got warmer Charlotte and I took to the seaside, at Tisvilde, forests and beaches on the North Sea. We would drive to the top of Sjelland at Tisvilde for day trips, which included nude bathing, and lovemaking in the sand, or on the forest floor. It was truly memorable and remarkably private. On one of our hikes through the forest we came upon a ruin of a cloister and an execution place from the eleven or twelve hundreds. It was properly detailed with a sign showing its original construction. There were a few of the original stones still standing. It was creepy to think about the time of witch hunts and the like.

In May my hotel contract was renewed, and I was learning new material, but drinking became a problem. The bar maid collected the excess draft beer in a large container, and insisted I drink it at the end of the night, which I did, like a fool. By the time I stopped playing at the end of May I was drinking regularly, a bad habit that stayed with me my entire time in Denmark.

In July the Copenhagen Jazz festival occurs in the first two weeks, and I got asked to play at the Bolten's garden on the 16th and 17th. This time I got on a poster along with notables from the rock and jazz world, although I was not playing jazz, strictly speaking. I played two afternoon sessions for about an hour and a half each. It was fun and it paid well. It gave me a lot of exposure.

I went up to Tisvilde after that and got a gig playing the Hotel Hojbohus or the "high life house." I got a room over night Saturday and a wage, to play on the veranda, a dream job that lasted about a month. After that gig I was out of work. I had quit the Kommandanten for the SAS Royal, and for some reason I didn't go back. I needed a rest from playing solo. I hooked up with Jacob Bacharach, a young jazz bassist, who I played with briefly while at the Salt and Pepper. We rehearsed some rock and pop tunes to work small clubs with a drummer, named Anders. We got some gigs, and played with Anders in the center of town, called "centrum." I bought some new equipment, a pair of massive Cerwin Vega Speakers and a sound board with sixteen track mixer. Jacob and I got along very well, and sometimes even played with my Roland drum machine as a duo.

By the end of 1991 work seem to evaporate for us, and I started thinking about other things to do. I had an opportunity to get a stipend to study in the Adult Education Division.

I could take "Danish as a Second Language" and computer basics. Starting in winter of '92 I started classes, on Peter Vedelsgade, and although I was accused of being distracted by my teacher, because being a music star weighed heavily upon me. I constantly had feelers out for music work, and occasionally got some, one night here and there. But I would have been better off using the time studying Danish. My goal was to be admitted to Adult High School the following school year to study about 55 hours per week with a nice State stipend. With a Danish High School diploma I could matriculate into university, all paid for by the State of Denmark.

But, I had to give up music as a full time career to accomplish this. I tried to keep in touch with Jacob very slightly, but did no more gigs with him. He was now focused on Jazz, and getting good with it. Charlotte was in her last laps with the Academy, and would graduate in another year, maybe two.

XIX

HIGH SCHOOL AGAIN, STOR TUBORG, BORNHOLM

In the Fall of '93 I matriculated into the Adult High School called "Efterslaegten", meaning "Ancestors' School," in Bella hoj, Copenhagen. The first weeks were pretty confusing for me, since only Danish was used. The exception to this rule was those young folks who wanted to practice their English. I befriended two kids half my age from my Chemistry class, and spoke English to them for the most part. They had grown up with American and British films, and they spoke with American accents! One of them was a Lebanese immigrant, who had an uncle living in Boston, USA.

I started this year with Psychology, Computer Science, Danish Literature, Art, Chemistry and Business Economics. It was quite a load, and required hours of reading in a language not my own. To say I got tired out would be an understatement. I fell asleep before Charlotte came home from school, before nine PM some nights. I usually took a "Stor Tuborg", a "Big Tuborg," in English, in the afternoon to relax after classes were finished. This habit of drinking a pint became a tradition for me, and I was addicted to it, like so many Copenhageners. My bike ride to Bellahoj was about three miles, a lot of it up hill. Bellahoj meant "beautiful height" or "hill," and the school was on a height, one of the few in mostly flat Copenhagen. I had sold my VW, and was driving my Eddy Merkx racer with books bungee strapped to the rear rack of the bike. It was efficient, since I carried all my books with me each day, and it was quite a load. I gained a few pounds with the travel and the beer drinking. I ate in the school cafeteria, but usually packed a sandwich from home. It was a pleasant school day, all in all.

My Art teacher, Fleming Lipholdt, was a known Danish artist, and he conveyed a lot to us about sketching, perspective, and water color painting, the most difficult. He taught me to do an etching in acrylic of the big tree outside school, which I dubbed "Efterslaegten's Trae". I used to stand with several beers purchased from the local kiosk, and sketch my tree for hours at a time. I loved Art. We also studied the history of Art in this class, very informative. Riding home after sketching and drinking was a reverie of sorts, and I usually lied down and tried to read, when I arrived home. Charlotte was staying later and later at the Akademiet, sometimes arriving home at eleven PM. We had the weekends together, and the summer before the school year, we took a vacation in the island of Bornholm in the Baltic, with Charlotte's friend from the Socialist party, Grete. Her mother loaned us her cottage there for a week. It was fascinating being on a Danish island that was once occupied by the Russian Army during the war. The beaches were rocky, and the water was cold, but there was plenty of sunshine, quite distinct from Copenhagen's cloudy weather.

One night hanging out in the local tavern in downtown Bornholm Charlotte and I got talking with a big man about Russia, who bought us drinks all night It seems that after the war Bornholm was threatened by takeover by the Russians, and they considered who to seek help from to maintain their identity. They thought first of Sweden, but no, Sweden would probably maintain an attitude of neutrality. They chose Denmark, now supported by American armed forces. Our new friend had a brother killed by the Russians after the war, and was extremely friendly toward Americans, hence the free drinks. By the time we were ready to leave we could barely stand to start walking, so inebriated were we. We finally got to the road that lead to the hills and forest along the shore line. It was pitch dark, we tried lighting matches to see, but we kept falling down on the path. Somehow we managed to get back to the cabin, and then had a big fight, about cleaning up the cabin, emptying the refrigerator, instead of lying down, which is all I was capable of at that point. She was adamant, it was time to leave and time to clean up! I forced her into bed and violently made love to her, and then we got to sleep. What a hang over we had after that night out! We ate brunch and beer with Grete's new friend, Carston, and then we cleaned up and made ready to go back home. First though, we went over to Carston's house for a big salad and who knows what? I know we ate a lot of garlic in the salad dressing. I think we ate fresh fish picked up at the market. It was a nice dinner, hosted by an original inhabitant of Bornholm. We also ate smoked fish in town at the local smoke house, freshly smoked cod from the North Sea. It was very tasty.

Back at school I designed a computer program to help a student learn vocabulary in a unique way. It was in Pascal programing, and it allowed you to deposit a phrase or word from one of your books into the program, and later retrieve it by author's name and page number, thus enabling the student to see the phrase or expression in its original form with the translation to English. I called it the "electronic wordbook", and it served me well, with all the books I was reading in. The program gave the author, the book title, page number and line number where the phrase was found. This contextualization really helped with learning the language.

At year's end came the exams. They were written, and oral before teachers other than your own, or from other schools. They were called "Censors," and they could be tough. In Art class we had an exhibit of all our work around the year. The whole school could see our work, as well the Censors and our instructors. In Chemistry I did my exam on light theory advanced by Isaac Newton. In business I analyzed the annual report of Basf Europe. In Danish I did a research paper on mores of the 1940's, and an unwed mother's struggle to avoid discrimination. In Psychology I drew a question or two about Kinnicot's work. I passed most of my exams, with the exception of Danish, which I got a very low grade on, and I had to file a grievance about, and lost.

After the embarrassment of losing my appeal of my Danish exam I was ready to throw in the towel. Although it had been a good experience for the most past, I wanted to go on "bistand", Danish for welfare. And it actually paid more than my student stipendium. I was shocked, to say the least. Looking back I wish I had stayed with school, and possibly retaking Danish. I wasn't thinking, I was drinking, instead. I believe I was suffering a case of depression from the loss of my music career, but failed to recognize it properly, and I had no psychotherapist in Denmark, but I should have.

XX

VACATION IN JYLLAND, JAN AND BERIT

Entering the summer of '94 we learned that Charlotte could take her final exam and be eligible for graduation. We decided to take a vacation to Jutland, that I like to call Jylland in the original Danish, pronounced "You-land." We were invited to a summer place owned or rented by Berit's boyfriend's parents. Jan was a schizophrenic who took medication, smoked a lot of cigarettes and drank beer regularly. The beer in Denmark has a parallel in France in their wine, something that children start drinking already at about age fourteen in both countries. Although alcoholism is a serious problem in Denmark there are still many Danes who drink beer regularly with no ill effects. I 'm afraid I was not one of them. Once I drank I changed, like the Swedes who come to Copenhagen, and are found drunk on the street corners, because the drinking rules in Sweden are so strict. The common expression went " keep Copenhagen clean, send home a Swede". I wasn't drunk on the street corner, but my intake was constant during our Jutland vacation.

We took our bikes, and me my wagon on board the train, but when we arrived the wind and the cold in June was forbidding. We sent our bikes back home on the train before our departure. When it rained the weather became really miserable. I soaked my shoes, then in my inebriated state, laid them on a gas heater only to burn them up nearly. I could still wear them but the fire had taken a big bite out of one shoe. We visited with Jan's parents, and they drove us around to some interesting spots, like the Viking grave hills, large mounds the Vikings dug to place their dead and treasures under. They stood sometimes twelve feet high and two hundred feet across ! What a work of landscaping! Some of the farmers in Denmark would like to excavate them to make for more usable land, but the government holds them as heritage sights. It was certainly a cold June, requiring coats and scarfs.

When we traveled out to the Atlantic near the resort area known as Skaegn, the water was most violent and the wind most high. There was an agriculture museum we passed along the way that had farm implements back a thousand years, and was intensely interesting to me. Seeing plows back to the stone/flint age were something extraordinary. We visited Horsens, a modern town nearby that had a silver museum with examples from all the great smiths back several hundred years. Along with it the new building also had modern art, which I guess didn't impress me, with the exception of Bille. I got a book about his art, but don't remember any of the rest of the artists in the exhibit. To end our visit with Berit and Jan we ate a big dinner at Jan's parents' home. We traveled back on the train with Berit and her two dogs, Siberian huskies. We got back to the main station where I had an argument with those holding out bikes. They wanted some outrageous fee for transporting them. I lost the battle, and had to pay the amount- I don't remember how much it was, only that it was unreasonable

Back at home everything was as usual with Klaus and Eva Nordso upstairs having marital difficulties, with Klaus leaving home, while Eva took up with a violent actor named Storm. He beat her up and we had to call for an ambulance for her, while Storm barricaded himself in the apartment upstairs, refusing to answer the door. The police should have intervened but we never called them. We felt that Eva should be the one to call the police, and she never did either. Somehow her affair with Storm ended shortly after that, and Klaus and she were reconciled. Klaus and his brother Mikkel had a popular acoustic flamenco band in Copenhagen, and Klaus stayed busy with his Conga drums, Mikkel on guitar, plus another guitarist. They had records and toured, but I don't know what happened to the Nordsoes.

1994 was also the summer that we received a visit from Grant Von Brumbach, a musical friend from the eighties. I knew Grant in Salisbury and we played in a duo for a short while. He was a great composer of pop tunes, but he frequently relied upon me as an

agent to get him performing work. Whenever I found work somewhere he would come around behind me a steal the jobs from me. I don't know how he was able to talk the owner out of hiring me and my band, and switching to a solo act instead. Maybe it was the money, I don't know, and I never confronted him about it. I just seemed to let the resentment I felt smoulder inside me, and when he came to Copenhagen I just let him get gigs wherever, I didn't help him, in other words.

He played in some clubs in town and made a good deal of money. I was drinking heavily while contemplating new music work. Of course the two don't go together very well, and I never found any work. This was my last year in Copenhagen, as we would be going to the States in June of '95. I attended a lot of the '94 Jazz Festival, and drank a lot of beer with it, gaining weight all the while. Charlotte was so busy with her last year I guess she just didn't notice what I was doing. We took hikes in and around Tisvilde, and visited art museums in North Sjelland on the weekends. During the week I spent endless hours in the Danish National Museum (of natural history) studying stone age man in and around the Baltic and Scandinavia. It was quite a sweeping history the National had, reaching back 245 thousand years! The Viking artifacts and peat bog men were the most interesting.

XXI

BACK TO THE STATES, PETER 69

Charlotte and I visited Kurt and Carmen with regularity in this period and I'm afraid to say there was plenty of drinking associated with those visits. Half the year in '94 seems like a blur to me now. The first half of '95 was occupied with preparations to leave Denmark. selling everything of any value, including all my music equipment, packing up all our belongings for shipment by sea, all took a good deal of time. I attended an exhibit of Johan Thomas Lundbye that really knocked me out. His was National Realism, but always impressed me as truly Romantic. I bought a slide show presentation of his major works which helped me with future music presentations. I was able to go to the library and photocopy all sorts of classical guitar transcriptions. I was able to find Bach, Rodrigo, Gaspar Sans, Gulliani, Sors, and Albeniz, many, many more. I gathered as much up as I could knowing that in the United States I would have to buy it to get copies of it. I also bought a new classical guitar from our friend Marianne. It was a hand made George Washburn from Chicago, Ill. I still have it, it plays well.

Instead of afternoon tea I was still with my Stor Tuborgs, usually two of them. I would gather the empty bottles for redemption at the corner store, get a few crowns to help pay for new ones. It was a regular ritual each afternoon, Tuborg beer, the tastiest beer in the world, made with hard water. In the Spring of '95 I had advertised our goods for sale in the "Blue paper", a free advertiser in Copenhagen. By about May we had our fight tickets for about a thousand dollars, and were ready to take off. We found a new tenant for the apartment, a young man who inherited my nice bicycle, the one I cobbled together from parts found down in the cellar dump of old bikes. He also got my carry wagon to hitch along with the very comfortable bike I made. Ah, I miss them, and hope he got out of them as much as I did in the several years I grocery shopped with that nice rig. Into that wagon went a week or two worth of provisions- it was roomy. Fully loaded the ride was smooth like glass, and not at all stressful.

Around early June 1995 we booked our flight to the States, and said goodbye to everyone we knew. It was bittersweet, our departure, so much to leave behind, and so much ahead. Charlotte had our cat, Freja, shipped, I think, in the cargo hold. We flew over the North Pole, and views from above were spectacular. We landed for a time at Rejkevik in Iceland.

I remember that well because I bought a cup of coffee for about six dollars! We got back up in the air about three hours later, and saw the land masses of Greenland and then of North America, all brown and sinewy. It was quite a sight!

We arrived in the daytime, and were detained in Customs and Immigration for several hours, while they checked out Charlotte's papers. It was amazing how long we were held there, but I guess that's the way it is for all foreign nationals coming into the U.S.. When we finally got released it was the middle of the afternoon, and I bent down to kiss the pavement outside the building. We met brother Neil, who agreed to collect us, and take us home to his house. We were pretty jet lagged, but slept good for the night, and awoke less frazzled. We left North Baltimore the next day and started driving to the Maryland Eastern shore. We met my parents and went to dinner at Lombardi's Pizza, Salisbury, and all was good. They were happy to see us after all these five years of my absence. We went home to their house on Ayers Lane in Snow Hill, Md., where we stayed for two weeks while we found an apartment in Snow Hill, as our home base.

We had amassed about $4500 from all the belongings we sold, and from our earnings: Charlotte worked as a nurse assistant after graduation last year, and was able to bankroll a good amount. I started working as a security guard with Bennett Security, and we interviewed for an architect position with Becker Morgan, and got turned down. Charlotte found an architectural draftsman job with a smaller firm for almost minimum wages, something like $5 per hour, but it was a start. I got a full time job working at the Salisbury Dresser-Wayne Pump plant on College ave. My aim, however, was to work as a substitute Teacher for the Wicomico County Board of Education, which accepted me once again. Then, after getting fired from Bennett on trumped up charges of not doing my duty by a tense supervisor named Pete Sturmfeld, I got back to work in the new school year, as a substitute. At the same time I took up course work at the Salisbury State college to seek teaching credentials for Social Studies Teacher, secondary school. I started right away in the Fall, and we became pregnant in November '95 with our son Peter Erik, who was to be named after his deceased grandfather, Peter Lerche, a well known journalist from Copenhagen. I took my first education course that Fall semester in the Foundations of Education, and interesting perusal of the history of education in the United States, and of the main laws guiding education. I got an A, so I made a good start.

By this time we had moved from the apartment in Snow Hill, and found a small house to rent on Sharp's Point Rd..in Salisbury. For the next nine months we both worked our jobs, me with school system and Charlotte at the drawing office. I also went to school studying education. When Charlotte's water broke on June 6, 1996 we were both at the Sharp's Point Rd house, outside on the front steps. It was time to go to the hospital, which we did, right away.

Dr. Kearney, her obstetrician, met us there and labor began. Around three o'clock AM the next morning Peter was ready to be born, and he came out without problems. He had reddish dark hair, and big dark blue eyes, quite different from the blonde with light blue eyes he became months later. When she became about eight months pregnant the drawing office laid her off, actually in violation of State law. We didn't fight it, but were not at all happy about it.

On June 7th, 1996 Peter was born, and the day after he was ready to come home.

School had ended for me and I was seeking summer employment with Wilkens Security Agency. I got a dream job at the baseball stadium where they played double A baseball. I was posted above the hill where the children played. It was a grand baby sitting operation! Charlotte brought our new son to the games, and it was nice. I got hit by a fly ball, had heatstroke once, and rescued a six year old from a bad nosebleed by carrying him to the aid station. Petey loved being outdoors, and was a quiet baby. My time at the stadium was a happy one with one exception: at home we had a problem with the neighbors two dogs, as they barked all night. This made it impossible to sleep the few hours we had between feedings of Peter. I complained to the neighbor, whose house was less than ten paces away from our house, and the sheer volume of the two dogs in their pen was too much. He said " why don't you close your windows and turn on air conditioning?" He obviously didn't give a shit, and we didn't want to use air conditioning, and didn't have any window air conditioners. The dogs were bad enough, but we also had a litter of cats outside the bedroom window making noise meowing. To top it all off our neighbor, who I'll call Glen, burned a 500 watt halogen lamp over his back door, directly into our bedroom. We asked him to turn it off after eleven, but he chronically would forget to turn it off. I bought a bb pistol to scare away the cats. I then decided to complain to the Wicomico District Court about a public nuisance, the dog noise all night. It was not my intention to swear out a warrant for Glen's arrest, but rather to have issued a so-called "show cause" summons, to get my day in court.

It would be just like small town Salisbury to issue a warrant for our neighbor's arrest on noise violations! I later learned that they did just that, hauled him off to jail, and made him post bail. Despite all that, the noise did not improve, and I started to record the dates and times that the dogs disturbed our rest. It was a whole calendar month, and I carried that to the court commissioner to further complain. This time when I got there I was arrested for "wreckless endangerment" charges, among others. I was supposed to have shot my bb pistol at his kids' windows, and into his dog pen. I was locked up with a $15,000 bail, which after a night in the Detention Center with illegal immigrants, I was bailed out by my mother. Over night I was interviewed by a Corrections Officer who asked me "how long have you been using drugs?"

Naturally, I felt humiliated by the question, and could only say that I wasn't using drugs. Then they drew blood to test me for AIDS. They were thorough, I'll give them that. It was middle afternoon before I got released. I retained an old colleague of mine from Parole and Probation days, Henry Vineyard, who suggested I immediately post "no trespassing" signs all over my place, which I did. The State Policeman who came to the scene noted in his report that "no bb's were found inside the dog pen" or near the windows, but the young State's attorney still wanted to prosecute the case. Vineyard was handed the bb gun, and he tried to shoot it into a Time magazine, and it didn't even break the paper. He negociated with the State's Attorney, and after charging me with about $6000 in fees, got the case dismissed, with the proviso that we neighbors didn't fight any further, and left each other alone. What an expensive tempest in a teapot! Peter's first three months were action packed, alright! Now impoverished by a lawyer, we set out to get ahead, but how? At least my bid to become a Teacher was no longer threatened.

We soon got notice from the landlord that we were not the kind of tenants that he needed, and were asked to move. We found a house to rent on a chicken farm on Hammond School Rd. in Salisbury. It was smelly, but quiet, basically nice with two bedrooms and an attic. While Charlotte was out working I lied with Peter on a blanket on the floor, and watched him learn to flip himself over on his stomach. At this time I was on a steady diet of St. Pauli Girl beer, about $250 worth a month. By 1997 I was well established as a substitute teacher, and I started to look for work playing the guitar. I found a part time gig at a place called the Cactus Taverna in Salisbury, usually Sunday evenings, for about $40 a night. I was not feeling so good about this job, probably because of the drink, but I carried on doing the same, despite. I was addicted to St. Pauli Girl, a decent German beer. I also started back teaching with Salisbury Music, and found one very bright student, Brandon Bernstein. At the same time I started taking more teacher credential classes at the

Del Tech branch of Wilmington University I decided to teach guitar at Delaware Community and Technical College. I had classes with half a dozen students, and it went well. If I hadn't been drinking so heavily I could have made more of this opportunity to teach and play. One morning, on August 4, 1997 I was awoken by my mother at about 6 AM and told that my father was possibly dying, and was being taken to Peninsula Regional Hospital. I showered in a hurry, and made it over to the hospital only to be told that he had suffered a massive stroke, that a blood vessel had burst inside his brain and had killed him.

The doctor said it might have been hereditary, a genetic predisposition. I went into the place where his warm body had been taken, and stroked his chest, talking to him for the last time.

Then I went to a restaurant with my mother to have breakfast. She ate cream chipped beef on toast, and she said that comforted her. There was no comforting me, and although I didn't always see eye to eye with him, I was going to sorely miss him.

I went back to play at the Cactus Taverna, and with a deep sadness played the best I could. The funeral was held at St. Francis de Sales Church in Salisbury with a caravan following the hearse all the way to the cemetery in south west Baltimore, where he was interred. I remember my brother helped me buy a new suit for the funeral, it was dark brown. It cost about $70, and Bob paid the whole thing, including a new tie and socks.

Peter was baptised at St. Francis the year before and uncle Mike and aunt Peggy were chosen as god parents. Peter was given the middle name Peter Erik Lerche Buchness. He was given his middle name in honor of my best friend in California, who phoned me back in '95 advising me he had been incarcerated for about three years for "conspiracy" to commit a drug deal. Some things never change....Perhaps this time Erik had learned his lesson and was going straight? I don't know, we haven't communicated since then.

Our life on Hammond School Rd. was quite pleasant: I was working for the Wicomico County Schools and Charlotte, the Salisbury Nursing home. I was running regularly, despite drinking beer to relax. My weight was picking up as a result of the beer drinking, and I was becoming robust in figure.

I remember our first trip from Snow Hill to Salisbury. I drove out the old Poweville Rd. to stop at the "Mad Russian's" place where there was a pond to swim in, and the old Russian didn't mind if people came to swim, so long as they didn't leave trash. Seeing the pond again after five year's absence was exhilarating, and I dove in paying no attention to possible obstacles in the water, and I rapidly swam across to the other side. Charlotte walked around the pond to meet me, thinking I was a little crazy, but I was manic, no doubt about it. There were things in the water that people had dumped, spoiling the pristine atmosphere there always seemed to be here. It was an omen for me of the area's changes in the past five years. I wondered if the so-called Mad Russian was still alive, or if he still owned the property. I'll never know, I guess.

Back st home on Hammond School rd. our next door neighbor was another kind of mad Russian, a Ukranian Peter came to call "Mr.K," from the name Konziola. Peter loved this old couple next door, and visited whenever he could. The old man was about eighty-five, and his wife was a few years younger. They were prisoners of the Nazis during the war and had stories to tell us, most of which I have forgotten. Old Mr. K was as mad as the Hatter, and regularly went outside with a 30-30 carbine and shot at the gatherings of birds. Then he would try to mount his farm tractor against his son's wishes, and they finally went to court over it to get Mr. K separated from his precious machinery. It was obvious to all of us that his days of running the tractor were over, but he still wanted to try. It was not long after that he died leaving the old lady with the farm and house. We visited her a few years after we moved from there, and she was still baking the Ukranian sugar cookies Peter was so fond of. She was in pretty good shape for her years, and I guess she went into a nursing home later.

In January '99 I received a letter from the Wicomico Board of Education that I was being let go due to a number of "negative incidents " reported by staff and schools in the district.

I called the principals of eleven schools to find out the nature of these complaints, but not one of them could provide any information as to complaints anyone had against me. Oh well, I had to chalk it up to politics, and let it go. I took a job with Radio Shack, first in Salisbury, and later in West Ocean City. I learned to sell cell phones and computers, and until I had a conflict with the young and incompetent manager, Tony Steel, things were more or less okay. Later that year('99)

I was asked to work on new Year's Eve to do inventory, which I refused to do, at which time Tony said he "had the authority" over me to make me do this. I told him he did not "have any any fucking authority " over me. He fired me for that remark, and I complained to the district manager, who backed up the firing. My next stop, Walmart, in Berlin, Md., where I found an electronics department manager job. The problems in that little department were more than I could stand, with the majority of them coming from the photo concession, which needed a better system, which I tried unsuccessfully to remedy. After about six months I was burned out. At the end I was called into the store manager's office to ask me why I was taking home the handheld computer home with me (?). That was the straw that broke the camel's back, and I handed my sweat soaked vest over to the female manager saying "here, that's my sweat, I quit."

I left the store, and never returned until I got a call from them that I had an $800 overtime paycheck sitting in payroll for several weeks. I had completely forgotten about it. That was August,1999, and I responded to an ad asking for an electronics "lead" at the Salisbury Staples, which I answered and got. In the meantime my education as a teacher was on hold, while I solved people's electronics problems. One plus was I was able to buy computer games for Peter and me. The internet was coming on strong, though dial up, as well as the sex scandals with President Clinton. Peter sat in my lap to play "Pajama Sam", and we had a great time with the mouse and the joystick. I had a great time with the bottle of St. Pauli Girl, and my consumption was up to about $250 a month, a lot of money for that time. I had given up writing for the paper, which was under new and incompetent management. The Salisbury Daily times was no longer worth reading, there was never any content, and it has not improved since that time until today. It is really a shame, because it was at one time an interesting paper with a maximum utilization of local talent and content. That was the period under the management of Mel Toadvine and Dick Fleming, managing editor, and entertainment editor, respectively.

Staples tried to promote its company as a "youth culture," and they hired excessively immature managers in their operations management. I ran into one of these, a nondescript twenty-one year old named Brent White. One day while exiting the men's room he shoved me by pushing me in the chest with his hands to get by me. I responded by calling him a "small nazi prick." He then wrote me up for offensive language, despite his aggressive behavior. The general manager saw fit to fire me for it, and there was no discussion about Brent's pushing and shoving of employees. That got me unemployment, and the opportunity to drink more. About the same time We bought a five acre former farm with six outbuildings including a barn. We were able to get it for a little under $100,000. We moved to this place with no central heat in January, 2000. It had a wood stove and I purchased an old 1982 ford pick-up truck and started hauling wood from the surrounding clear cut forest. It was exciting, but the house remained cold, and we all got colds and flues. I especially contracted a bronchitis that wouldn't leave me for about six months, despite many antibiotics. The wood stove got us through the winter, with a lot of smoke problems, and creosote build up in the stove pipe. I took it apart and cleaned it out, but foolishly continued to burn pine in it, so it repeated the same problem. It was not until I paid Steve Rallye to clean it, and starting splitting my own oak, that the situation improved. During this time I started having depression, which no doubt was caused by excessive drinking, so I sought out help from the Joseph House free clinic in Salisbury, and got referred to an old geezer psychiatrist named Mc Farland, who gave me plenty of Zoloft. The antidepressant worked, but gave me high blood pressure, so I stopped taking it after a couple of months. Talking with Mc Farland seemed to get me nowhere, except into discussions of the Andrew Wyeths he had hanging on the walls of his office. I asked for another psychotherapist, and started seeing a clinical psychologist by the name of John Zweig, who seemed to help me, although I don't remember the content of our discussions, so he must not have helped too much. I asked for yet another therapist, and ran into Mark Walsh, a young psychiatrist who had me pegged for a schizophrenic. I took his assessment back to John Zweig and he concluded his diagnosis was like "putting on a parka in the summer time." I dropped Dr. Walsh after that, as I did Dr. Zweig, shortly after that.

I applied for substitute teaching with neighboring Worcester County, and got hired in early 2000. I substitute taught at Stephen Decatur High school and Middle school, as well as the Berlin intermediate school, grades K through sixth grade. I continued playing the guitar at the Cactus Taverna for a limited time, my classical was pulling hard on me and they wanted rock music at the Taverna.. The pay there was unforgivable, so, I quit.

I stopped drinking, and started running more seriously. The new job with Worcester was working out fine, and I continued my teacher credential courses, and I could see daylight at the end of the tunnel. I found an additional teaching position as a GED instructor with the Westover, Md. Correctional Institution, teaching mathematics. It was twelve hours per week in the evenings Monday through Thursday. It was a good gig, until the day school teacher found peppermint wrappers on his classroom floor after my nights there. I had thrown away all trash into the trash cans, so he must have taken it out and dropped it on the floor as evidence for the Principal. It was a violation of prison protocol to give anything to inmates, so I got reprimanded.

I also got criticized for the best teaching practices I was using, and which really got good results.

Come August 2001 I was tired of the games being played, and I decided not to renew my contract with the prison school. Instead I found a long term substitute teaching position at Stephen Decatur High school, in Algebra I. It was my first professional teaching post, but in an area other than my own certification, but I was enjoying teaching math, so I gave it a try. On September 11th the World Trade Center Twin Towers were hit during my second period class, the ninth graders. The next day I was informed that I was being taken off the class by the Principal, apparently something to do with behavior that morning of the ninth graders. My "class management" skills were called into question, and I was relieved of the class, but continued as a daily substitute. I missed the extra income, but as they say, I licked my wounds and moved on.

After Christmas of '01 I started looking around for other teaching opportunities, and came across a GED teacher wanted ad near Cambridge, Md., at Morningstar Youth Academy.

I interviewed and got hired starting February'02. I left Worcester County Schools in good standing, and started with Morningstar residential treatment center for the Department of Juvenile Justice. These were the badasses that the court ordered from the juvenile detention centers. I was hired as the Social Studies Teacher, but due to the shortage of math teachers I began teaching math, mainly because I was used to working with math. We had small classes, usually not more than nine students, though these boys were a handful. Most of them were former drug users, everything from heroin to cocaine and pot. Many of them had been sexually abused by their wayward parents or guardians. They were generally hostile toward authority, and reaching them in order to "teach" them required a lot of distractions. Early in the morning I would show them a videotape of the BBC morning news I had brought from home, and we'd discuss events and so on. They came to look forward to the morning newscast. Those who had come from tenth, eleventh and twelfth grades were mixed together, but ninth graders were taught separately. So, I generally had four classes of upperclassmen and one ninth grade class each day. My day was full of disciplinary actions, and there was a merit system governed by counselors, presumably with psychology degrees or similar training. They did not seem that effective to me, but I had to work *their* program. Failures in the classroom did not always reflect what was happening in the counselor's offices. Often bad behavior in the classroom was rewarded later in the counselor meetings. It was strange, indeed, but I had to live with it.

Some days I taught Math all day, some days Social Studies, and some days I mixed in Writing. I kept them busy with lesson plans each day, and we were not bored. I also mixed in physical exercises for these boys who sat all day. We did Kempo pushups, and a variety of Tai Chi and Yoga things I had learned over the years. One month we co wrote a news letter called the"Blade" after Walt Whitman's "Blades of grass". It was a great success, and the whole school got copies to read their stories about the 911 terrorists, and what must have motivated them to give up their young lives to destruction. I brought with me an aging IBM computer to teach them Lotus 1,2,3, and other early programs to get them interested in data collecting. In the late afternoon we often had movie time, where I brought a relevant recent film and they watched it with a follow along sheet to stay focused on the meaning of the film. In any case, we stayed busy.

Boyce Mosely was my Principal, and he was always supportive of the things I did. He was often absent from the school, but he was well liked by the boys, this 75 year old black leader, who talked to them at their level. He was very effective at reaching the boys.

I met my coworker, Anita Brown, here at Morningstar, though she was brought on board after I was, and we became close friends. She was a certified Math teacher who loved teaching as much as I did. She lived in nearby Fruitland on Clyde ave. with her African American husband (she was originally British). We were able to ride together to work some days. We lost touch after she moved to a teaching position in North Carolina.

My Morningstar hiatus has a bittersweet conclusion, in that I was fired by Mr. Mosely, who heard from a small conspiracy of senior students, who claimed that I said "Fuck Mr. Mosely" in reference to a chain of command matter. I never said such a thing, and tried in vain to convince Mosely of it. He went with the boys, and decided to terminate my employment in my ninth month on the job. I later pleaded with Director, Derrick Witherspoon, to sign an approval for a satisfactory school year of work for the State Department of Education. He agreed, and I was able to get my student teaching obligation satisfied thus. One way to satisfy a student teaching obligation in Maryland was to substitute a *school year* of satisfactory teaching from an accredited school

Elvis Presley's father, Vernon Presley, once remarked to his son, that there were three elements to a happy life: Someone to love, something to look forward to, and something to do. I was out of work, but I loved my wife and child, I had my teaching certificate to look forward to, and a barn roof to repair. Besides that, I got a healthy unemployment check to pay our bills.

I was about to enter a sabbatical from work for a number of months in order to look around, and take a breather. On my way home from Morningstar for the last time I stopped by the Hyatt Regency Hotel on the Choptank, to ask for music work. It so happened they were hiring, and I got a week contract to play Friday and Saturday night. What a disaster! I wasn't ready to play solo in such a big venue, and didn't have the amplifier for it. It paid nicely, and I played the best I could, but the bartender didn't like what I played, and that was the end of that. It was a good learning experience, but I was not asked back.

The old barn had a gaping hole in its roof on the south side, which admitted rain down into the hay stall. It was shingled with asphalt shingles over the original Shaker shingles that were nice cedar splits. I draped a light blue tarp over the hole and tacked it down, and thought about what to do. I had some plastic fencing from an above ground swimming pool left by the Banks. It was printed with images of Scoobie Doo the dog. I rolled it out on the roof on the blank side, and started hammering it down as new roofing. I lapped it clapboard style down the roof, and it looked pretty good. I improvised a skylight in the middle of it with a large plexiglass window that was for the most part water tight. I finished up screwing down the plastic, as I had developed carpal tunnel syndrome in my forearm from the percussive action of the nailing. I needed to see a Chiropractor, and that was when I met Dr. Louis Oeschli, and he fixed the carpal tunnel syndrome over a couple months. The roof was finished, and it was time to spray paint the barn and the house. I bought a cheap spray rig at Walmart and started to applying the housepaint. It worked well at first, and I got the barn done. By the time I got to the house the spray mechanism was clogged, and became useless. I had to buy a new one, and it too got blocked up, so that was it for the spray operation. To spray paint a house I discovered one needed a serious and expensive spray apparatus. I was ready to go back to substitute teaching, and it was 2003 in a hurry. I started applying for teaching positions for Social Studies, but there were none to be found. I returned to Worcester County schools, and could only get work at Snow Hill Middle School.

I got in tight with vice Principal Mike Pruitt, who gave me work at least three days per week, enough to get by. Charlotte had moved over to the Peninsula Medical Regional Center hospital, and Peter was in Fruitland Primary school. I practiced the guitar with the rest of my free time, and was into some interesting new classical guitar pieces, including Vals number 4 by Barrios. I had major ambitions with my guitar study, most of which disappeared over the next few years when I began playing church music at St Francis de Sales Catholic church, around 2009.

In the meantime, however, I was searching for new psychiatrist, while still drinking a limited amount. I was overweight and running now and then. It was at this time that the country experienced a real estate bubble and my property gained in value, so I took out a second mortgage to get through the sparse work periods. I worked on the property all the time, mainly cutting all the fields, and trying to make it look luxuriously green. The surrounding property owners decided to plant pine trees where there were clear cut forests and fields. So, we experienced the growth of a Federal tree farm around us.

I met Dr. Fred Dittmer in about 2003, his having moved down here from a metropolitan area on Maryland's western shore. He was a unusual psychotherapist, in that he had a master's degree in Public Health, as well. He was convinced I was an ex hippie drug addict (which I certainly was not), and he prescribed Neurontin for me to calm down. He thought I suffered from Bipolar Disorder Type II, and thought I had manic periods. I was seeing him for depression, though, and didn't necessarily agree with his diagnosis. He made a good impression on me, however, and he was the all-fatherly type I needed since my Dad's death. His method was that of the traditional psychotherapist, who took hand written notes, and listened very carefully to what I said. I saw him once a week for a long time, fortunately I was a dependent on my wife's health insurance, to pay for it. This was also the time when I discovered my high blood pressure, and began seeing Prakash Dalal, the Indian

Cardiologist. Without medication my blood pressure hovered about 165 over 90, but soon came down to normal with medication.

Sometime in late 2003 I took a job in security with Bennett, my old employer. It was working on a Construction site, at the Glen Riddle Estates, a hoyti toyti land development scheme just outside Ocean Pines. The construction crews, with few exceptions, were possibly illegal immigrant Mexicans, Brazilians and Guatemalens, all experienced framers and builders. My job was to provide some quasi police presence, and make sure all the guys wore their construction hats, or their body harnesses when up on a roof. This took more work than you might imagine, but I was finally able to "discipline my troops." I saw all the houses go up, all of them in the $400,000 price range or above. They seemed like a rip off to me, as they were hastily built with inexpensive materials, like plastic trim boards. This was the peak of the building-real estate boom, and prices were vastly inflated. In the Spring of 2004 the job was over, and we were all laid off, promised new positions within the company. I accepted a 4PM to11PM shift at the Perdue Headquarters in Salisbury, and it seemed alright at first. There were some "odd balls" working there, however, and I had started running again, and liberally stretched my legs in the office complex when no one was there. I was discovered doing this one night, and I got into a hassle with the number one "odd ball", and the supervisor fired me. It was okay, because I wanted back into education, and out of security work that paid nominally. So, I started back at Snow Hill Middle school, where I stayed for the next five years.

So I lost another full time job due to my "behavior", and Charlotte thought it was time for me to talk with Dr. Dittmer about some more medication. Now, I knew I was never psychotic, but Dittmer recommended I take a minimal dose of the antispychotic Risperidal, to help control manic states. It took some tries, but I finally settled on 2 milligrams per day, which I've taken ever since. Charlotte felt that it helped, and that it changed me subtly. I guess she was right, but I didn't notice any changes. By the summer of 2005 we had worked a good deal on our property, and had it in fairly good shape. Charlotte's mother, Carmen, came to visit with a friend named Lilly, and we went over to Assateague island for the day. Charlotte and I were running together at this point, and we took about a three mile run up the island and back. Everything was nice. We came back home in the late afternoon when expresso coffee was served. I drank a cup, and shortly after that I was stung by a wasp. I felt an initial shock, as I became severely startled, and headed into my bedroom to lie down. I passed out, urinating in the bed, and paramedics were called, as there was the suspicion that it was caused by the wasp sting. I was administered Epipen as a precaution, and taken over to the emergency room. I came around again at the emergency triage area, where I woke up shivering in the cool air. I was shaking violently from the chill, and at last taken to a hospital room, where a nurse tried to give me a spinal tap, but said that due to the unusual arthritis build up in the low spine they couldn't take it. Apparently I had a low grade fever, and they wanted to test for meningitis. My blood pressure had dropped to about 90 over 50, so they wanted to know what blood pressure meds I was on. I told them it was a combination of nifedipine with beta blockers. The Cardiologist judged that I had suffered "neurocardiogenic shock" probably brought on by the abrupt bee sting. In my mind there may also have been some effect from the strong cup of expresso. My pulse had dropped to somewhere abnormal, possibly from the beta blockers, which I found out later, may lower the heart rate. Later when I met with my cardiologist, Dr. Dalal, I complained to him that my pulse rate has always been on the low end, and he recommended that I have a pacemaker implanted in me. He said that the pacemaker would govern the heart rate at 60 beats per minute, and keep it there. This way if my heart rate dropped enough to make me pass out, it simply would not happen due to the 60 beat per minute control in the pacemaker. It sounded reasonable, and I agreed to have it installed a little while later. About a year later I had another syncope episode, and it was attributed to the blood pressure medication I was taking, Norvask. It was changed back to nifedipine.

In 2006 Carmen came back for another visit, and she complained of chronic indigestion. We all packed up for a weekend in New York City and took off in our late model Ford Taurus. It was September, and the hotel rates were low. We stayed in midtown Manhattan, and went out to eat in a Viet Namese restaurant, and had a delicious meal. Then we walked around until late. We got up early next day and went to the Metropolitan Museum of Art for several hours. I wanted a poster of the Bruegel painting of harvest, but decided at the last moment not to for some reason. It was only $20. While we were in the museum Carmen insisted on taking Peter with her, but I wanted Peter with me to survey all the art in the place. Carmen was complaining of stomach pains, and rolled around in a wheelchair. Little did I know it at that moment that she had a stomach cancer that would kill her in the next year. If I had known I would not have preempted him from her. From the Met we moved on to the Gugenheim Museum of Modern Art, also nearby. We saw all the modern pieces hanging there, and were impressed at the architecture created by Frank Lloyd Wright, with its circular staircase like floors.

We ended our outing with a bus ride back to the hotel. It was very modern and comfortable, quite unlike the crowded bus rides of my youth in the fifties. Before we went back home we did stop at St.Patrick's cathedral, and looked over all the ornate altars. It was a beautiful cathedral. Peter was particularly impressed; he thought it was "pretty cool". We took Carmen to the airport, telling her to have her stomach looked at. She agreed, and when they had a look they found cancer in her esophagus. In the winter of 2007 Charlotte booked a flight to Copenhagen to see her mother for the last time. She died in hospice care shortly thereafter. When Charlotte traveled back to the States she was still alive, though in bad shape. We learned of her death by telephone from Jan, Charlotte's older brother. It was a sad beginning of a new year, March, 2007. Charlotte's small circle of a family had been broken.

I received my Teacher Certificate, but found no vacancies for social studies teaching in any of three surrounding counties. In fact, I never did find a job through one expiration of my certificate in 2009. I continued substitute teaching at Snow Hill Middle School, and kept practicing my guitar. I stopped into St. Francis de Sales church one afternoon to talk with Bill Alexander, a fellow musician I had interviewed for the paper in the eighties. He was now the Music Director for the church. I showed him a videotape of a guitar concert I had recorded with photographic slides a few years ago. He invited me back with my guitar, and I played up in the choir loft for the first time. Bill was impressed, and agreed to hire me to play alternate Sundays, Bach and sacred pieces transcribed for guitar. I was very nervous the first time I played, but as the weeks went by it got easier, and my repertoire increased. I got a nice salary for the two pieces I would play every other Sunday. The feedback from the congregation was positive, which made it all the more worthwhile. We developed a unique way of playing: Classical guitar with organ in the background. It sounded very nice, and in 2013 we recorded a CD of sixteen such pieces.

From sixth through eighth grade we enrolled Peter at St. Francis de Sales school. It was expensive, about $4,500 per year, but I managed to get assistance from the diocese for needy students, making our contribution about $2500 per year. Peter was happily playing trumpet with the small marching band led by Mike Robbins. They were rated 14th nationwide for a small ensemble. We marched with them when they played the parades in Salisbury, Pocomoke and Hurlock. It was great exercise, and sometimes very much in the winter cold, but worth it. It was fun to march alongside these twenty youngsters while they played amazing pieces. Each year they gave an indoor concert too, where they played themes from Exodus to James Bond's numbers.

Peter got a good musical education doing this, and he learned to read basic music, and understand theory. During these years, 2007 to 2010, I devoted my life to children, my own as well as those at Snow Hill Middle School. Charlotte worked at the hospital caring for patients, while I took Peter to all the things of his young life. My time at home I spent learning new hymns for classical guitar for the communion and offertory services at the masses. Peter's three years in middle school were good years for us, punctuated only by a casual observation by Principal, Mark Record, that Peter seemed "withdrawn" from other students, starting about the end of seventh grade. He was interviewed by a guidance counselor, who thought he was pretty normal, and we didn't think much more about it until he entered tenth grade, when it became more pronounced.   Peter graduated from the eighth grade at

St. Francis with an award for the "best artist" in his class, and entered James M. Bennett Senior High as a freshman, where he lettered in track, having thrown the shotput and the discus. He had a close friend, Brandon Pittman, who he shared his track experience with. Peter had a fairly normal first year in High school, and he rode the bus to and from school. It was near the end of his sophomore year that Peter experienced problems with concentration. He was assessed for attention deficit disorder and given a counselor, Mr. Collins. I started taking Peter to the Wicomico Mental Health clinic to see a psychiatrist and a social worker. After about a year of counseling the doctor advised us that Peter showed signs of schizophrenia, but never gave him that diagnosis. Into his junior year Peter started expressing feelings of hostility toward his parents, and we thought it was just teenage rebelliousness, which in fact it wasn't. Peter took over the guest bedroom, and started isolating himself up there after school. He was administered Vyvans, a form of ritalin for ADHD. After about a year of taking that he experienced a psychotic breakdown, and in his senior year had to be hospitalized at the Adventist Childrens' Hospital in Cambridge, Md. He had experienced two prior visits to the emergency ward at Peninsula Regional Hospital, which were inconclusive. This admission kept him for 21 days, and he was given an antipsychotic called Abilify, which slowly stabilized him. He was taken out of school for the last two months of his senior year, 2014, and therefore did not graduate with his class. It was a tough experience visiting Peter in Cambridge about twice a week, and to see him in his helpless state. When he was released in May he was assigned to a partial hospitalization program at Community Behavioral Health Center in Salisbury, where he spent from 8:30 in the morning to 3:00 in the afternoon. He received intense psychotherapy, and slowly started doing better, getting more in touch with himself. This was 2014, and Peter was on his way to normalcy with medication, which to this day he has remained.

We must return to the year 2013, which was traumatic all around for my family.

One night I had pain in the abdomen all night long, and went to the emergency room in the morning, where it was discovered I was having acute appendicitis. They operated that afternoon, and took a biopsy of the infected organ to discover I had a malignant cancer in my colon. I had an operation to remove my right colon, then I was to undergo chemotherapy for the next six months, twice a month at the hospital. So, for six months I carried a sack with a chemotherapy pump for a few days every other week. The nausea was the hardest part, and I took medication for that. By October it was over, and I tested free of the obvious signs of cancer. I had the side effect from the chemo of the numbing of my hands and feet, so my guitar career was cut short. I could not feel the strings properly under my fingers. I have the problem to this day. My two mile runs had to stop also because of the foot numbness. It has been two years I have been in remission, but the numbness has not changed. They say sometimes it takes years, so I am still patient and hopeful. Fortunately, Bill and I recorded our music CD early in 2013, before I had the side effect of numbness, but my performing at church had to stop, and I sorely miss it.

On November 29th of 2013 I got up with sharp chest pains, and had to ask Charlotte to take me to the hospital, where it was ascertained I was having a heart attack. I had a blockage in my heart and had to get a stent installed. Charlotte believes that this heart attack was another side effect of the chemotherapy, but I don't really know. No one can say. Anyway, as a result I suffered congestive heart failure, and my breathing was short, I had to be administered oxygen through the night and into the next few days. I remained in the hospital for about a week, but when I got home it was recommended I return to the hospital because of the congestive heart failure. I was released after about three days, and sent home with a visiting nurse, who checked on me about once a week for a couple of months. Finally, I was seen by a pulmonologist, who cleared me of the congestive heart failure, but the year 2013 lived up its name as an unlucky number.

I stopped substitute teaching at Snow Hill Middle School when a new vice Principal named Christine Welsh became the administrator of substitutes. She hand picked her own people, and I was let go. I complained to the Principal, but to no avail; I never heard back from her. My former boss, Mike Pruitt, once warned me that it was a women's club at that school, but I didn't take it seriously at the time. I should have. I found a new part time job working for Chesapeake College teaching English as a foreign language to immigrant populations on the Eastern Shore. This lasted about six months, and the Adult Education program was taken over by Wor Wic Community college, and I was out of a job, but now content to be fully retired. The one exception is that I care for my 87 year old mother one day a week, take her to lunch and doctor appointments, and generally have a good time with her. I get a small stipend for this, which helps with the bills.

My future life will include going back to GED teaching through Wor Wic Community College, and reworking my poetry, some of which I have included at the end of this memoir. Looking back now I realize that I began my adult life after I created the following nature meditation for myself, and I'd wish to pass it on to others. Every morning I awake to sit in a quiet spot, and before I sip my hot coffee I silently recite and meditate on the words:

XXII

NATURE MEDITATION

Quiet, as in the pine hollow, among the pines
Still, like the mountain pond, suspended between the peaks
One, as with the earth, as with the earth's magnetic core
Rooted, like the tall Georgia pine trees, erect, seeking for light

Then, I sip my magic elixir, which coffee has always been since the day Joe Palermo first introduced it to me all those years ago in scouts. I am glad that I am sober nowadays, and free of pot, just on a natural high, with my three times a week swimming 22 laps in the Olympic pool at the local YMCA. By the grace of God my cancer is in remission, my blood pressure is under control, and I 've found a good psychotherapist in Dr. Jay Harkhani, an Indian psychiatrist. Peter is going into the Community College this Fall, and Charlotte still enjoys her job as a Patient Care Tech, working with patients in the post surgical ward. Every other week I cut several acres of grass, and Charlotte tends both vegetable and flower gardens around the property. Peter has his own small truck and his driver's license. He hopes to be working soon, although he has never had a job, other than volunteering at the hospital.

In the 1960's as a teenager the only thing I wanted to be was a poet, and maybe a bit of a songwriter. Here, I conclude with some poem meditations from those years.

POEMS

The Lone Gull

The lone gull loves to soar
Chirping his call to me and unbothered
By his fellows, resuming his fall.

Just before night he is loudest
As though this blanket cloth for sorrow
Wraps his daily existence on the edge
Of his harmonies, which are praises only
To himself.

Each day harmonizes with the next,
The chance for changing views unrestricted.
Never longing is the life of the sea bird
So light but so steady, at darkness
He finds the peace we are still searching for.

San Francisco 1970

Calico Kitten

Muscles twitch
Desert flowers at sunset
In openess of African fauna
The Panther seeks my spirit
And upset by not knowing
Why, but knowing which,
She lingers, little thing.

Berkeley, 1969

Breath

Breath, believe it, the wind does not cry.
Shadows reveal it, sing songs in the sky.
Stolen minds unreel it, stolen moments make it fly.

Breathe, and control it,
Laugh, and unroll it.
Let the dead drift with it,
Learn to unlift it....
Breathe....believe it, the air does not grieve it.
Let the blood receive it, hold it in and keel it.

The desert sands....
Each crystal understands....

San Francisco, 1971

The Market St. I know

I look at the sky above between the buildings.

Here, waiting for the car, that sky is a crimson copper.

The red, yellow and white city lights shed

Their appearances on it.

How much like the sea it looks from between

This valley of banks and business houses!

The clouds and the fog, and then,

This shroud of smog differ from the sea,

Only in the latter's infinity.

Church st. station, San Francisco, 1966

Sunset

O silent straights of gray
Whose magic lies in melancholy
The deep, deep waters.

O strands of silver
Wrapped on crimson and blue,
On an infinite background
Of space.

A tear of fire
Dropped into the ocean
A moment ago.
Leaving us a sort of
Screaming glow.

Sunset district, San Francisco, 1966

The Dissatisfaction of the City Dweller

I cannot go this cold night down green and dark pastures
    And sniff the algae of neighboring forests,
Nor the odor of goldenrod of the fields nearby,
    Nor listen to crickets in this tall green grass of nature.

I cannot enjoin myself to the music of fertility in the
    Ground here, beneath the moon and stars.
I cannot leave here because I am bound with
    Your haters, O nature.

I, your lover O nature am bound
                To run,
                Along pavement.

San Francisco 1967

Schools for *NOLEARNING*

Like the sad

Eyes of a school bus

My vision flares

In the images of

Confusion I behold.

Quickly they fleet away,

Raising the past, and

Returning my politics,

To my pockets....

San Francisco 1971

The Secret

In the battle of dreams I fought feelings
Frightful like the tiger's claw.
The real world came to me again like the tiger's teeth
Falling into waking, floating like the lily pad...
Alone in a pond overgrown.
Down and down I fall with the beats of
Splashing pounding reality-reverie.

Like swimming through a dark wine
I hold my teeth to the surface though,
And the Godsend of understanding
Wrestles with the restless illogic
That turns its tales, and roll on its rails
Which are we, unawares.
It spins and winds, winning and whipping us.
Till we find difficulty feeling that it is not Illusion.

Fear blows its ice cold breath on my breast,
Threatening me with sudden death,
And making me think I am not here for these
Verses only, and virtues seeming vices
And the viciousness of ignorance returns
In waking wildness, as the supreme command.
And consciousness coils from the evil
Turning inward to the lanes of safety.

San Francisco1967

Poem Meditation on Leaves

The leaves don't complain
Though they be plucked at intervals
From one another, on the branch.

Each one receives light, and for some,
It is filtered through all the others:
Each one receives light, tho' it be filtered
Through many others, on the tree.

They twist and turn in the wind
And sometimes become loosened from
The branch, unable to find their way back,
Once they drop.

And even though life remains in them
For a brief period they are nurtured,
All alone, in space,
With the radio waves of the sun to
Sustain them and the moisture in the air
To preserve them.

And when they fall
They fall gracefully in the air,
Cushioned on currents.
     No wonder they don't mind
     Being put to the ground.

The route to the top of the tree is
Long indeed,
The sun there, not impeded and from which
Point draws all the nutrients for the
Survival of the tree.

God sees the tree there,
And the human race
Is given a reminder.

                    Dedicated to the survivors of the Nazi
                    Holocaust Salisbury, Md.. 1979

The Wife Song

Someday I'll go running down this road of life
Singing a beautiful song about my beautiful wife,
And each day I'll thunder over the grave of
My wondering yesterdays. And every night
I'll lose myself mending my ways.

Oh, into the waters of life I must go once again
Growing stronger than my body, so used to its pain,
Lost and still winding through my glorious lives
I'll send gentle mists for all the sweet wives.

                    San Francisco, 1970

Demi-Haiku

The wind and rain subtly separated
Against the leaves flowing full,
Their veins to loose an image
Of moisture brought for all
To cleanse and renew,
Remould and review.

From showers to layers
Layers to logs and debris
In roads and streams, half mess, half beauty,
Come sun! And set me free.

Bolinas laudromat 1970

END